This is number two hundred and eighteen
in the second numbered series of the
Miegunyah Volumes
made possible by the
Miegunyah Fund
established by bequests
under the wills of
Sir Russell and Lady Grimwade.

'Miegunyah' was Russell Grimwade's home
from 1911 to 1955
and Mab Grimwade's home
from 1911 to 1973.

MAB

The world of Mab Grimwade

THEA GARDINER

THE
MIEGUNYAH
PRESS

THE MIEGUNYAH PRESS
An imprint of Melbourne University
Publishing Limited
Level 1, 715 Swanston Street, Carlton, Victoria
3053, Australia
mup-contact@unimelb.edu.au
www.mup.com.au

First published 2023
Text © Thea Gardiner, 2023
Design and typography © Melbourne
University Publishing Limited, 2023

Every attempt has been made to locate the
copyright holders for material quoted in this
book. Any person or organisation that may
have been overlooked or misattributed may
contact the publisher.

A catalogue record for this book is available
from the National Library of Australia

Front cover image: Russell Grimwade, Mab
propped up on a fence, 5 August 1912, black
and white print, Sir Wilfred Russell and Lady
Grimwade Collection, UMA 2002.0003.00703

Designed by Pfisterer + Freeman
Printed in China by 1010 Printing Asia Ltd

9780522878905 (hardback)

For my mother, Susan

Contents

Introduction

On 4 January 1887, George Colman Kelly wrote a letter to his sister-in-law Margaret Weatherly, to inform her of the birth of his first child:

> I have been presented with a daughter and a pretty little thing she is with an unusual quantity of very dark hair. Aggie got through it all splendidly and the baby was born very healthy and strong. Aggie is wonderfully well, so much so that the Doctor says it was almost unnecessary for him to be calling every day.[1]

Agnes Dalziel Kelly, or 'Aggie', gave birth to her daughter in St Kilda, Melbourne. Agnes and George named her Mabel Louise Kelly, after her paternal third great-grandmother.[2] Mabel Kelly, or Mab as she preferred to be called, was the only daughter and the eldest of George and Agnes's three children. Born into a genteel family in colonial Victoria, she lived her life within the boundaries set for a woman of her class. Her status enabled her to benefit from the opportunities available for genteel women, including a large inheritance, private education and frequent travel.

In many ways Mab epitomised her class and generation, yet she was astutely aware of the responsibility that her class, wealth and status afforded her. While some Australian women were able to enter the public sphere in the first decades of the twentieth century, rendering them 'exceptional' for their time, Mab happily occupied her role as Mrs Russell Grimwade and, later, Lady Grimwade, rarely testing the parameters of her gender or her class. While her

Opposite, Mab gardening at Miegunyah, October 1916.

marriage to the Victorian chemist, botanist, industrialist and philanthropist Russell Grimwade has defined her public narrative, she was a multifaceted and interesting woman in her own right.

Those who knew Mab invariably describe her as having been caring and generous, a good dancer, strong-willed and occasionally austere. According to various accounts from family members, what mattered most to Mab was her loved ones. While she and Russell were unable to have children, a fact that greatly saddened the couple, Mab was very close with her immediate and extended family. Younger members of her family recall her as an attentive and stimulating companion, eager to escort them to interesting performances and places. Described by her niece-by-marriage Camilla Kelly as 'thin, small [and] neat [and] very active till late in life', Mab was energetically engaged with all aspects of her world.[3] Photographs reveal a stylishly dressed and well-postured silhouette; she was rarely photographed without a hat or a string of pearls. She held an extensive collection of A-line dresses, leather gloves, lined cashmere cardigans, printed silks, furs and crisp collared blouses, many of which are housed at the National Gallery of Victoria, donated via her estate or through the Art Foundation of Victoria by Mab herself. She is depicted at the wheel of a motor car, reading quietly in the garden, walking in nature, reclining in a Venetian gondola, and holding her beloved Scottie dogs.

Born on the eve of Australian Federation and passing away in the early 1970s, Mab lived through tumultuous shifts in Australian society from the comfortable vantage point of her expansive estates and elite social circle. The society she was born into was one of promise and technological innovation, of boom and depression, of heightened nationalism and wavering imperial ties. Tracing her life allows for an examination of broader social and cultural contexts that illuminate several aspects of Australian history during the late nineteenth and early twentieth centuries. Mab's narrative can tell us about the culture of gender and class during this period, Australians travelling abroad, the role of women in Australian philanthropy, the status of women in Australian sport, the development of rose-naming practices, and the importance of gardening in the national imagination. Mab was not a passive subject of cultural and social phenomena—she helped to shape the world in which she lived.

Opposite, Arnold Shore, *Mabel Grimwade*, 1937

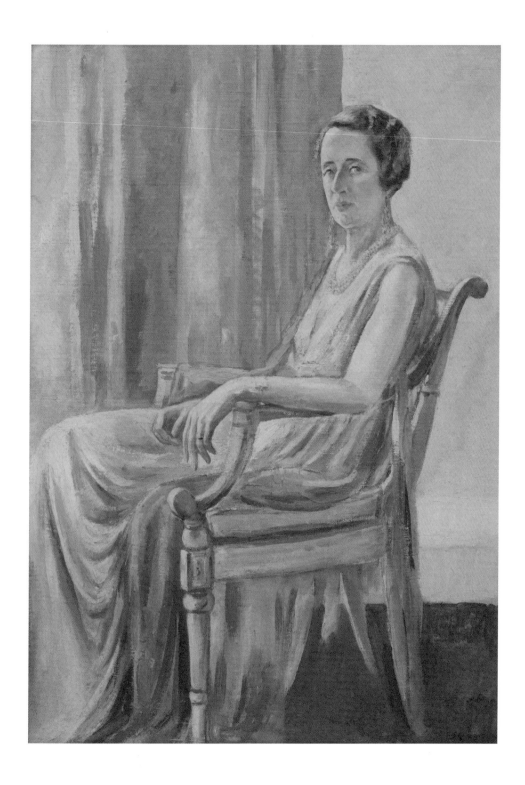

Mab channelled her energy into a variety of interests and activities and was an active participant in Melbourne's social and cultural life. As a member of Victoria's social elite, she was among those who felt a personal responsibility to help forge the future of Victoria. Mab was involved with extensive philanthropic and charity work, most notably serving as the president of the Fitzroy Mission Free Kindergarten. She exercised her abilities for leadership, administration and event planning through organisations and committees that she both sustained and supported. As a conservative nationalist and a loyal member of the British Empire, she was associated with various cultural and civic institutions formed to preserve imperial ties and foster Australian culture, such as the Victoria League for Commonwealth Friendship, the Royal Horticultural Society, the National Trust of Australia and the Native Plants Preservation Society of Victoria. Outside of philanthropy, she enjoyed a variety of recreational activities, many of which were the pastimes of the British aristocracy. Participation in such activities as golfing, polo, tennis, horse racing, motoring and gardening was both a source of enjoyment and a performance of class and privilege. Her social calendar was filled with art exhibitions and openings, theatre and ballet performances, race meets, polo games, charity events and open gardens, which she attended and organised.

Mab and Russell's homes—'Miegunyah' in Toorak and 'Westerfield' at Baxter, near Frankston—were the centres of the Grimwades' social and familial life, and an expression of their interests and tastes. Miegunyah in particular was a dominant shaping force in Mab's reality and imagination. She occupied its rooms and grounds for much of her adult life; its structure, contents and gardens were the physical manifestation of her and Russell's national and imperial identities, and the couple's desire to create a living artefact that would preserve their way of life. While Miegunyah and Westerfield provided Mab with a sense of permanence and a physical tie to her beloved home country, she and Russell were frequently called beyond national borders, eager to experience different cultures and expand their large collection of furniture, art, Australiana and botanical specimens.

Given Mab's significant contributions to Australian cultural life, it is surprising that no published account devoted to her life has existed until now. Her absence from the historical record reflects the general marginalisation of women in Australian history, where the dominant narratives centre the stories of men and the nation. Indeed, Russell Grimwade is woven into national histories, his name synonymous with scientific innovation and patronage, entrepreneurship and formidable philanthropy. While his contribution to Australia is undeniable, Mab is often overshadowed by her husband and by the Grimwade name in the brief historical accounts of her life. This book belongs to a century-long legacy of attempts to challenge these prevailing narratives by telling the stories of Australian women. When we recover the lives of women such as Mab Grimwade, we are able to re-examine the very core of Australian history and see the past through a fresh lens.

While Russell Grimwade left a large private collection—including auto-biographical papers, letters and miscellanea—that could be accessed by his biographer, John Poynter, Mab preserved very little in the way of personal papers. Searching for the imprint of a woman's life is a challenge repeatedly expressed by the biographers of women. Mab appears to have been the architect of her minimal archival record, a secretive family atmosphere among the Kellys encouraging the absence of personal documentation. As a result, Mab's own feelings, thoughts and opinions are relatively inaccessible to us. The archive is not a record of objective truth but a repository of what was deemed valuable to preserve, or what was incidentally left behind. My task is to make sense of these remnants of a life and forge from them a cohesive, truthful narrative.

In researching this book, I devoted much time to scouring the social pages of the daily press, gleaning a hint of a personality from formal correspondence and family archives, locating Mab's voice in brief travel diaries, and searching for a glimpse of her character in numerous photographs. From the late nineteenth century the social pages of Victorian newspapers furnished reports on the glamorous lives of Melbourne's genteel classes. The activities of 'Miss Mabel Kelly' drew the attention of columnists as she attended social occasions and captained an all-girl cricket team in her youth, while reports of 'Mrs Russell Grimwade' and, later, 'Lady Grimwade' focused on her generous patronage of various societies and clubs.

Although Mab is described by her surviving relatives as having been a regular correspondent, there is very little evidence of this. Some personal letters have been preserved in family archives and the Grimwade Collection at the University of Melbourne. Several letters written by Mabel Kelly to her immediate and extended family during her teenage years provide insight into her girlhood interests and personality. We know that she was a patron of many causes, a committee member and president, yet the records of the institutions with which she was associated contain no correspondence from her, and their minutes of meetings give no account of her opinions.

The extensive papers of Sir Russell and Lady Grimwade, held at the University of Melbourne, include scant traces of Mab. However, the few letters, travel diaries, long lists of bills, subscriptions, donations and bank statements hint at her daily life, her interests and observations, and the causes she championed. Travel diaries illuminate her shifting identities as an Australian and an imperial subject sojourning from the peripheries to the centre of Empire during the twentieth century. A certificate from the Royal Automobile Club of Victoria recognising her 'special services rendered to the Club and to motoring generally' reveals a lifelong passion for motoring and automobiles.[4] The inclusion in her papers of a publication titled *The Elements of Home Nursing* issued by the Red Cross Emergency Service, with handwritten scrawls pencilled on the pages and 'M. Grimwade' written on the front cover, encapsulates her commitment to charity work and volunteering during wartime.[5] These snippets provide crucial, albeit often mundane, fragments of her life.

We are fortunate in having an extensive collection of photographs, some from the Australian press but many more taken by her devoted husband, a highly skilled photographer. While such images provide invaluable insight into Mab's domestic, social and public life, they reveal more about how she was seen by her husband and by journalistic photographers than anything of her own vision of her world.

The fragmented nature of the available sources and the resulting gaps and silences in our knowledge of Mab's life have dictated the structure of this book, which attempts to form an account of her through the traces of what she left behind. At the same time, this account explores how her family history, her interests, activities and movements elucidate the time in which she lived and the society she represented. In the words of historian Barbara Tuchman, biography is a 'prism of history'; individual lives can act as conduits to wider historical themes.[6] While the first chapter provides a biographical sketch of Mab's familial background and her marriage, the subsequent pages privilege the thematic over the chronological, offering a series of vignettes that illustrate the world of Mab Grimwade.

Chapter 1.

BEGINNINGS

Above, Studio portrait of Mabel Kelly 1902.
Following spread, Mab and the party at
Woolongoon, September 1908

'The bride wore a lovely gown of ivory white satin, and her hair was very prettily banded with silver net and a small cluster of orange blossom.'

PUNCH 1909

In 1908, 21-year-old Mabel Louise Kelly was confronted with a life-changing decision. In the summer of that year she had met 29-year-old Russell Grimwade at Woolongoon, a property near Mortlake, Victoria, owned by her relatives the Weatherly family.

Russell was handsome, well educated and, by the time he met Mab, involved in the substantial growth of his family's pharmaceutical business, Felton, Grimwade & Company, as a partner and the director of its new research laboratory. The young entrepreneur had been invited to Mortlake by a former Ormond College friend, Sol Macpherson, to join a party of guests at Woolongoon comprised of Sol, Mab and her cousins Violet and Gladys Weatherly. Accepting Sol's invitation, Russell travelled from Melbourne to Mortlake, crossing the dusty plains of western Victoria in his Tarrant motor car. During their stay at Woolongoon, the party enjoyed a few weeks of shooting and socialising while Mab and Russell's relationship developed.[7]

The couple announced their engagement a few months later, only to break it off the same year. John Poynter, Russell's biographer, suggests that Mab's refusal to marry Russell was because she had second thoughts,[8] but other sources intimate that her father was the reason for her hesitation. George Kelly appears to have objected to Russell because he derived his income from 'trade'. While Russell's inherited wealth was derived from the scientific innovation and entrepreneurialism of his father, the Kellys' wealth had been generated by the spectacular success of their early investment in the Broken Hill Proprietary Company (BHP). George's reservations perhaps masked his own less-than-respectable family history, a history he may have hoped would recede from memory with the passage of time.

THE KELLYS

George Colman Kelly was the first Australian-born child of the ten children of Louisa and John Kelly. Mab's paternal grandparents were among the flood of migrants to the Antipodes during the 1850s gold rush. John emigrated from Ireland to New South Wales in c. 1854, Louise following in c. 1856. The couple were attracted by the promise of a new start in New South Wales, its opportunities for social mobility providing a stark contrast to those offered in Ireland. While John was descended from wealthy Irish landowners from Galway, his family suffered financial loss during the Irish Potato Famine of the 1840s, which devastated Ireland, causing poverty, starvation and mass emigration. In the aftermath of the famine, John and Louisa lived in Balliansloe in eastern Galway on a family property, where they had six children. John held several administrative positions in Galway, making his living primarily as a tax collector. After becoming implicated in a lawsuit regarding the defaulting of payments, he felt that he and his family had no future in Ireland. They embarked on the journey to New South Wales while John was still on bail.[9]

John and Louisa Kelly's life in the colony of New South Wales was typical of migrants in colonial Australia, marked by a peripatetic lifestyle and quickly changing fortunes. Initially, John was employed as the first Sub-Collector of Customs at the Port of Albury, a position opened up by Victoria's separation from the colony of New South Wales in 1851. During his employment as a sub-collector, John was known as a 'diligent and dominating man', his meticulous assessment of duties payable on goods endowing him with the nickname 'The Gauger'.[10] After spending two years at Albury, he was appointed police magistrate at Deniliquin, where he became a respected and influential member of the community. While little is known of Louisa during this time, she appears to have been a strong-willed and capable character, proving herself adaptable to the conditions of life in the settler-colonial environment.[11]

By the 1860s, John had fallen out of favour with the Deniliquin public. His questionable past resurfaced and was made public knowledge, and additionally he was charged with misappropriation of public funds. As a result, he was forced to dispose of his property and belongings. He died in Sydney in 1866, his hopes for a better life in the settler-colonies unfulfilled. Louisa had left her husband three years prior to his death, moving with her children to Melbourne, where she opened a boarding house. The Kelly children had mixed fortunes, pursuing the financial opportunities offered in the settler-colonies. Louisa's eldest son, Hubert Hugh Kelly, having inherited his grandfather's Irish estate, became a wealthy pastoralist in New South Wales. His younger brothers Bowes and George were also drawn to the pastoral life.

At twenty years of age, George Colman Kelly was eager to make a living. After finishing school in Melbourne in 1878, he joined Bowes as a jackeroo and then a station manager in western New South Wales. In 1884 George met Agnes Wilson while he was working as an overseer and bookkeeper at Billilla, a large pastoral holding on the Darling River near Wilcannia in north-western New South Wales. Agnes lived at Billilla, having emigrated from Scotland to live with her married sister Jeanie Weatherly: perhaps Agnes was among the substantial group of single British women who had been encouraged to emigrate to the settler-colonies in the 1860s–1880s to find suitable husbands or paid employment.[12] If this was the case, Agnes succeeded in her mission. On 20 January 1886, aged thirty-five, she married George, twenty-seven, in the Church of England at Wilcannia. The wedding was small and private, attended only by Jeanie and her husband, William Weatherly.

In 1884 George and Agnes Kelly's lives took a dramatic turn. George's brother Bowes bought a one-fourteenth share 'in the syndicate formed to develop the recently discovered Broken Hill Proprietary Company's mine' and divided it equally with George and his brother-in-law William Weatherly.[13] Within six years, the £150 Bowes had invested in BHP had grown to £1,250,000. The wealth accumulated from the investment made station manager George Kelly into a gentleman. Such a dramatic shift in social status was possible in the colony of Victoria, divorced from the rigid class structure of Britain. In one generation, the Kelly family fortunes had been transformed.

•

George and Agnes's lives followed the trajectory of those Australians propelled into the genteel classes through investment. In the 1880s, the couple moved to 'Marvellous Melbourne', the wealthiest city in the colonies. The gold rush of 1851 had transformed Melbourne from quiet pastoral settlement to booming metropole. In the post-gold-rush years, a discernible cultural and social elite had developed in the city, supplanting the old gentry from the early years of colonisation. By the 1880s, George and Agnes Kelly had joined the ranks of this new elite. While George was 'of a very quiet disposition', he quickly became 'widely known and respected' among his peers.[14] He and Agnes adapted to the social world of Melbourne's aristocracy, attending balls, parties, theatre performances and concerts, and travelled extensively. This decade saw Melbourne at the height of its land boom as the city ushered in an era of industrial development, technological innovation and a growing urban culture. In a single decade (1881-91), its population increased from 268,000 to 473,000.[15] While manufacturing was steadily becoming the city's greatest source of income, the Kellys chose to invest their wealth in real estate, shares and large pastoral holdings across Victoria. Properties included 'Rosehill', a 529-acre (214-hectare) expanse of rich farming land at Pentland Hills near Bacchus Marsh, and landholdings at Mildura and Swan Hill. In 1908 they purchased 'Barwidgee' in Caramut, inland from Warrnambool, which would prove extremely financially beneficial to the Kelly siblings in later life. The properties were kept for livestock and racehorse breeding, while providing the reserved George with a country escape from the fast pace of city life.

From 1888, the Kellys lived at 'Glendearg' in North Brighton. Katrina Weatherly describes the expansive property where Mab spent the first years of her life:

> Drawing rooms, dining room, billiard rooms, five bedrooms, a nursery with a bathroom attached, and with the modern conveniences of both hot and cold running water. Three pantries, a housemaid's separate pantry and three servant's rooms meant there was ample space in the house for the kitchen, scullery, washhouse and linen press areas. An outside six-stalled stable with an adjoining tool room, harness room and coach-house provided ample facilities for George's horses. The stable and paddock beside the house meant the children grew up amongst horses and harboured a familiarity with the animals from the time they were very young.[16]

In July 1897, George and Agnes purchased 'Montalto', one of the largest estates in the south-east Melbourne suburb of Toorak, extending over 11 acres (4.5 hectares) in Orrong Road.[17] Settled by wealthy pastoralists, merchants and professionals in the 1850s, Toorak was, according to historian Paul De Serville, 'synonymous in the public mind with wealth, extravagance and display'.[18] The home at Montalto was originally built in 1856 for James Blackwood, a member of the wool-broking firm Dalgety, Blackwood and Co. The progression of the

Victorian land boom in the 1880s saw more elaborate mansions and grand villas built in the area, usually designed by pre-eminent architects. Reflecting this shift, the original dwelling at Montalto seems to have been demolished during the 1880s and the two-storey mansion acquired by the Kellys in the 1890s was much larger, occupying the land of 681–689 Orrong Road.[19] Agnes remained there until her death in 1931, more than twenty years after the death of her husband. This was to become a matter of some concern to her children, who questioned the wisdom of retaining a considerable staff to care for such a large house with only one occupant. This—the world of the wealthy elite—was the context in which Mabel Kelly spent her childhood.

CHILDHOOD

Over the course of her life, Agnes Kelly fulfilled her expected role of wife and mother. She gave birth to Mab's two brothers, Charles and George Dalziel, in 1889 and 1891 respectively. All three children were baptised in the Presbyterian Church following the religion of their mother. Upon marrying Agnes, George had severed ties with his Roman Catholic heritage. However, neither he nor Agnes was devoutly religious, and the Kelly siblings were brought up in a mildly religious atmosphere, attending Presbyterian services.

Mab and her brothers grew up in a world shaped by Victorian bourgeois values. Genteel children of this period were ideally raised in a sheltered domestic setting that encouraged Christian virtues. As the older sister of two boys, Mab would have been expected to model moral conduct for her younger siblings, and while the Victorian gender order presupposed male authority, elder sisters were often held in high esteem by their younger brothers. As members of Melbourne's bourgeoisie, the siblings received a formal education at private schools and spent considerable time abroad with their parents.

Mab enjoyed a privileged upbringing and spent much of her early childhood playing with her brothers and cousins, enjoying horse-and-buggy outings and countless social events. On one occasion in 1898 the Kelly and Weatherly

Following spread, House and garden at Montalto, April 1909.

cousins hosted a 'Juvenile Costume Ball' at Prahran Town Hall, where they entertained many of their young friends for a night of dancing Irish jigs amid an array of colourful and 'orientalist' decorations. Guests dressed in historical and classical costume; Mab came as the Queen of Roses, wearing 'green silk, made in Watteau fashion, trimmed with all kinds of roses'.[20] In the late nineteenth century, fancy-dress balls were a common social activity for children of the social elite in each colony. They were a microcosm of adult 'society', providing a contained and acceptable form of entertainment for young people.

In childhood Mab developed a close bond with her brothers, which endured throughout her life despite some periods of separation. Charles, the second-eldest Kelly, was educated at Melbourne Grammar School, leaving in 1906 to go jackarooing at 'Willow Tree' in New South Wales, and then at 'Greenhills' near Barwidgee. In 1915 he joined a cavalry regiment in England; he survived a gas attack during service in France and was awarded a Military Cross upon his return to Australia. He went on to manage the family properties of Barwidgee and 'Caramut North' (purchased by the Kelly siblings in the 1920s), turning them into two of the most successful sheep runs in Australia. Dalziel studied law at the University of Melbourne, later becoming interested in agricultural and wool industries. He was president of the Graziers' Association of Victoria from 1926 to 1928 and was ultimately knighted for his services to the Australian wool industry as chairman of the Australian Wool Board. After retiring from the Wool Board, he acted as director of several major Victorian institutions, including the Herald and Weekly Times Pty Ltd, the *Argus* newspaper, HC Sleigh Ltd, and Colonial Mutual Life Assurance Society Ltd.[21]

The Kelly siblings were a close-knit group; they often lived in physical proximity to one another and shared financial interests and a social circle. Mab, Dalziel and Charles were partners in Charles Kelly and Co., a substantial enterprise that in 1954 owned 50,000 sheep and 6000 cattle stationed at Barwidgee and Caramut North. While Dalziel sold his shares of the company in 1934 due to a disagreement with Charles,[22] Charles and Mab continued their partnership until 1962. Mab bought Caramut North and Charles bought Barwidgee, a decision that led Dalziel to believe Mab had taken Charles' side in their disagreement. While Dalziel alienated himself from his family as a

Opposite, Mab with Dalziel and Agnes at Montalto, December 1926.

consequence, Mab later re-established contact with him. Apart from this conflict, the Kelly family maintained strong familial bonds through to the next generation. Charles was the only sibling to have children, with his wife, Gwen Affleck, providing Mab with a lifelong connection to five fraternal nieces and nephews.

•

Less than two years after purchasing Montalto, the Kelly family and Annie, one of their servants, embarked on an international journey 'home' to Britain and Europe for three years. In the Kellys' case this meant Scotland, where Agnes was born, and they established themselves in Edinburgh. When the family set sail on 7 March in the SS *Ophir*, Mab was thirteen, Charles and Dalziel eleven and seven. It is possible that Mab acquired at this time the taste for travel that was so evident not only before her marriage and during her decades with Russell, but also after his death when she continued her frequent voyages.

In Edinburgh Mab was sent to a French school as a weekly boarder, and it is to that time that we owe a scant half-dozen letters written to her mother, two cousins, an aunt and an uncle. In this period it was common for Australian children from wealthy families to complete some of their schooling abroad, a privilege signalling a well-rounded education. Writing to her cousin Gladys, Mab described her daily life at the school in Edinburgh and her friendships there:

> We go to bed very early. We have no preoccupation after dinner. We have dinner at 7 o'clock ... I like Hope very much she is a boarder too, but she has since gone home for this week. She lives in Glasgow you know. Her Mother died last term. I am thinking of asking her to come to lunch.

It appears Mab was underwhelmed by the activities offered at her school, taking solace in the friendships she made and the breaks she spent returning to her parents and travelling the Continent. She signed off the letter to Gladys with a colourful and detailed sketch of two women wearing garments reminiscent of traditional Chinese court costume, revealing an early artistic talent and an interest in decorative design.

Some of Mab's letters were written from Edinburgh, others during brief visits to Paris and Interlaken in Switzerland. They are not models of style, and

Mabel Kelly to Gladys Weatherly, October 1901.

the one addressed to Gladys in June 1901 from Edinburgh in schoolgirl French suggests the fourteen-year-old writer still had a little to learn.

In her correspondence, Mab contrasts the mundanity of her time at school with the exciting periods she spends travelling with her family across Europe. She describes 'travelling about such a lot and having such a good time', staying in lavish hotels, shopping at Parisian boutiques, visiting art galleries and monuments, and enjoying the natural beauty of the Swiss and Scottish countryside.[23] The correspondence offers a glimpse into Mab's inner world: she is opinionated, discerning, and well versed in the formalities of letter writing. She expresses a love of all things French, proclaiming a distaste for Germany 'and any place where they could not speak French'.[24] The letters also illustrate some of what became her lifelong interests: picturesque scenery, walking in nature, photography, motoring, art and fashion.

One letter written in September 1901 from Lausanne to her uncle Bill (William Weatherly) gives some idea of the family's travels and her own observations:

> Father, Vi and I went on the Lake of Lucerne to Bergenstock [Bürgen-stock] and we got a little cable tram up the mountain. Another day we went to Flucken [Flüelen] by steamer and we were three hours going there, but the lake is so pretty and from Flucken we drove out to Altdorf to see William Tell's monument. It is a very handsome monument.
>
> When we were [in Lucerne] we went on a trip up to Schynige Platte. We went up the mountain in a little train with an engine to push. We had lunch up there and the waitresses were dressed in the native costume. They looked so nice. Father took two snapshots of them. Then after lunch Father and I climbed to the top of one of the summits near Daube. We had a most beautiful view of the Lake of Brienz and Interlaken. It was very hot climbing. From there we went to Berne. [We] did not like Berne it is a dirty place so we did not stay there long. From there we came here. There does not seem to be much to see but we have a very pretty view of Lake Geneva from our windows. This morning we went to the Cathedral to service. It is a very old place but it is being restored a lot then we went to have a look at the Castle and came home. Tomorrow morning we are going to Geneva. From there to Paris, Dieppe, London, Edinburgh to school.

Mother and the boys are at the English Lakes and they like it very much. I have no more news. Hoping to see you soon. We are coming out at Xmas.[25]

Throughout her correspondence, Mab exhibited a discernible desire to keep up with the latest European fashions. Writing in June 1901 from Edinburgh to her mother, she went into some detail about the high price of sealskins (some 33 guineas as opposed to the £14-20 she had expected), describing 'some very pretty black caraculs [a type of fur coat] for 12 & a half guineas upwards. They are all to be the fashion this yr & I tried one on & Nannie thought it looked very nice. Perhaps you wd see a caracul coat at Robertson's & so know what I am wanting to get.' A letter to her aunt Margaret from the Hôtel Saint-Pétersbourg in Paris in September the same year told her:

This morning we went out and I got such a pretty new hat for next term. It is a pale blue felt hat trimmed with pale blue velvet and feathers (plumes). I got it at Guillard Soeurs Avenue de l'Opéra. This afternoon after Father and I had been out together doing a little shopping while Mrs Weatherly and Vi rested. Then after tea I took them to the Bois de Boulogne. We were there driving round for two hours.[26]

Apart from revealing her early interests and observations, Mab's correspondence reflects the importance of familial connection for her. She uses informal names for all her family members, shows an unwavering affection for her mother, aunt and cousins, and speaks highly of her brothers and father. The letters are scattered with affectionate remarks, expressions of longing for the company of her cousins and aunt, and deep concern for any family member who has fallen into ill health. Her devotion to her family continued throughout her life.

When the family returned to Australia in February 1902, Mab was sent to a private secondary school, as was common for girls of her class. She is believed to have attended Oberwyl in St Kilda, a school to which George Kelly had paid the fees for his niece Violet.[27] The school, founded in 1867 and closed in 1931, was named by its founder, Elise Pfund (1833-1921), after the Swiss village where she was born. Mrs Pfund, née Tschaggeny, was an art patron married to James Pfund, who became Victoria's surveyor-general.[28] When Mab was there, the school was under the ownership of Isabel Henderson and Adelaide Garton. Unlike her two brothers, who rode their horses from Montalto to and from Melbourne Grammar School, it is probable that Mab was a weekly boarder at Oberwyl.

By 1906 Oberwyl was one of the largest girls' schools in Victoria, with an extensive offering of academic subjects, such as classical languages and mathematics, and subjects more commonly offered to young ladies. Here, Mab would have learnt the skills and social graces that constituted ideal femininity: music, singing, dancing, art, elocution, cookery and dressmaking were all essential to becoming a well-rounded dilettante. She would have also been introduced to gymnastics and physical education, a new area of female development that followed the formalisation of education in Australia.

Schoolchildren during this period were recipients of a transformation in the Australian education system that occurred during the second half of the nineteenth century; schooling became compulsory and central to the lives of children and adolescents. Following Federation in 1901, students were shaped as modern Australian citizens, taught 'obedience ... truth, honesty, self-reliance, industry, temperance and other virtues'.[29] Young unmarried women made up the bulk of the teaching workforce, as was the case at Oberwyl. Katrina Weatherly tells us that Miss Garton was a particular stickler for punctuality and accuracy, and that Miss Henderson 'stressed upon the girls the importance of orderliness in dress, behaviour and speech because she believed good grooming indicated proper personal pride and self-respect'.[30] Miss Henderson was to have a lasting moral influence on Mab and became a beneficiary of Mab's philanthropy and work with the Fitzroy Mission Free Kindergarten, later named the Isabel Henderson Kindergarten.

Mab finished her schooling at the age of seventeen or eighteen, having obtained a well-rounded formal education. She was versed in French, Italian and German, understood the principles of mathematics and physics and the intricacies of classical literature, had developed at least rudimentary musical and artistic skills, and was primed to carry out the duties of a homemaker. She continued to foster a busy social life, the social pages of the press revealing a seemingly endless series of dances, dinners, teas, sports games and other social functions. The same names crop up on many occasions, reflecting the relatively small social circle of those attending, many of them old boys or old girls of various private schools.

As her early twenties approached, Mab may have felt significant pressure to make some choices regarding the trajectory of her life. Women's employment opportunities were expanding during the early twentieth century in Australia, and prolonged schooling for girls provided opportunities for further education at university. However, the cultural expectation for genteel women such as Mab was to fulfil a domestic role as a wife and mother, preferably at a young age. At this important juncture, Mab met Russell Grimwade.

MAB AND RUSSELL

In 1909, almost immediately after returning her engagement ring to Russell, Mab left Australia with a friend to visit South-East Asia. Their departure was noted in *The Bulletin*:

> Two Melbourne girls make ready for a free and unchaperoned festivity on uncommon lines. They intend to 'do' Java, Borneo and Burmah in one comprehensive rampage. Justice Hood's pretty daughter Kate and her chum, Mab Kelly (the George Kellys' hopeful), comprise the valiant pair.[31]

As this quote intimates, Mab's decision to travel overseas unchaperoned by a male relative defied the contemporary social expectations that defined her gender. Such a socially unorthodox excursion suggests that the young Mab Kelly sought independence and freedom at this pivotal moment in her life. When she returned home, she continued to exercise her autonomy and resumed her engagement to Russell,[32] even though the female members of his family had ceremoniously ostracised her after she jilted him. Mab and Russell were married on 12 October 1909. Their wedding, held at Toorak Presbyterian Church, was a quiet affair attended only by relations and old friends of the bride and groom. It was reported in Melbourne's popular social magazine *Punch*:

> The bride ... wore a lovely gown of ivory white satin, and her hair was very prettily banded with silver net and a small cluster of orange blossom. The bridesmaids were Miss Freda Grimwade and

Mr. Harold Grimwade's little daughter, who walked before the bride both going and coming from the church, carrying a basket of roses. The bridesmaids all wore very pretty dresses of soft white satin with overdresses of silk muslin in pale blue patterned with tiny pink roses. They wore large white chip hats [handwoven straw or palm-leaf hats] trimmed with wreaths of skeleton leaves and tulle, and carried bouquets of pink roses. After the ceremony a reception was held at 'Montalto'. The rooms were beautifully decorated with white roses. A marquee was erected on the lawn for the wedding tea the tables for which were grouped with heath and roses. The toast of the day was proposed by the Rev. Dr. Marshall. The bride and bridegroom left early in the afternoon by motor for Macedon, where they will spend the honeymoon.[33]

At the time of the wedding, both Frederick Sheppard Grimwade, Russell's father, and Mab's father, George Kelly, were in poor health. While FS Grimwade was in attendance, George did not attend his daughter's wedding and Mab was given away by her brother Charles. George was, however, sufficiently well to greet his guests at the reception. He died prematurely on 27 December 1909 at the age of fifty-two; Frederick Grimwade died the following year. Mab and Russell had intended to spend their honeymoon in Europe in 1910, but the death of Russell's father delayed the trip until 1912. The couple enjoyed their honeymoon closer to home, staying with Russell's brother at Macedon. They spent the summer of 1912 in England, visiting relations, motoring, and attending aeroplane shows. They sailed home by way of New York and Canada, where they explored the Rocky Mountains.

In August 1910 Russell purchased Miegunyah, a single-storey house on Orrong Road in Toorak, a few hundred metres south of Mab's mother at Montalto, as a wedding gift to Mab, purchased in her name. The property originally occupied 2 acres (8000 square metres) of land in a newly subdivided area of Toorak, but it expanded over time, spreading to a second frontage on Selbourne Road that provided a sanctuary for its residents. Miegunyah itself was also developed substantially in subsequent years, and a second storey added to the home allowed Mab to wave from her bedroom balcony to her

Opposite, Miegunyah, August 1913.

mother at Montalto. In 1920, the couple purchased a second plot of land at Baxter near Frankston, which would become their weekend getaway, Westerfield. Mab and Russell spent over forty years of happy marriage at Miegunyah and Westerfield. Indeed, Russell talked of being 'one of the privileged and fortunate ones who has had a very long and very happy married life'.[34] Mab's niece Camilla Kelly recalled in 2019 that:

> They were a very devoted couple who adored each other. Aunt Mab definitely looked up to Uncle Russell & tried to do all she could to please him. She had a rather 'highly strung' nature & he was a very kindly and calming influence on her ... He was a very gentle and kindly man and always looked after Aunt Mab as if she was a delicate piece of Dresden china.[35]

While Mab and Russell did not have children of their own, Miegunyah was often populated with nieces and nephews of both the Grimwade and Kelly families, as well as several beloved Scottish terriers. In the absence of children, the couple pursued shared and separate interests. While Russell continued to expand his family's pharmaceutical empire to include industrial gas production, Mab maintained a sizeable household staff that included domestic servants, gardeners and cooks. She was also the orchestrator of the Grimwades' busy social life, organising charity events and social gatherings with Victoria's plutocracy. Outside of the home, Mab maintained her financial investments and built her stature in the philanthropy community, both presiding over and as a member of several social and charitable organisations. Her social consciousness was often combined with her innumerable hobbies, which included golf, horseracing, dancing, the theatre, art collection, painting, horticulture and gardening. Mab and Russell also travelled regularly within Australia and internationally. While their expeditions abroad sustained their appetite for exploration and provided additions to their vast collection of art, furniture, rare books, ceramics and other ephemera, they also reaffirmed their love of Australia.

Chapter 2.

AT HOME

'the advent into society marks the
fact that the girl had reached years of
discretion. Her school days are over,
and she is old enough to take upon
herself the responsibilities of life.'

ALBURY BANNER AND WODONGA EXPRESS, 1901

Mab entered adulthood as Australia was becoming a new nation, a circum-
stance that initiated a collective desire among white settlers to create a distinctly 'Australian' national culture. While radical nationalists sought to sever
ties with the British Empire, valorising the country's foundations in convict
labour and working-class organisation, Mab and her contemporaries favoured
a more conservative nationalism, maintaining strong imperial loyalties while
celebrating Australia's enterprising pioneers and its distinctive history and
culture. This romantic view of Australian exceptionalism, extricated from the
histories of First Nations people, was reflected in the Grimwades' passion for
collecting artefacts of the country's colonial past, and in the homes that contained their treasures.

The impulse to maintain and preserve a unique Australian culture that
simultaneously took pride in its imperial connection also found expression
in Mab's active engagement in fostering Victoria's vibrant social and cultural
life in the twentieth century. Over time, she developed interests in the arts and
philanthropy and helped to nurture and conserve various cultural, civic and
charitable institutions in Melbourne. For her Australia was home, and the
properties she shared with her husband were an expression of their national

Opposite, Mab playing with a young relative in Miegunyah gardens, 8 February 1931.

identity and the primary settings for their busy social and familial lives. While she was embedded in Melbourne's civic and creative circles, Miegunyah provided the space for her to extend these social networks, fundraise for charitable causes, and embody the role of wife and hostess. Home was also a refuge, a place for relaxation, gardening and spending time with family. Mab's domestic responsibilities at Miegunyah were considerable, requiring expertise in household management and event planning. In her young adulthood, she developed the skills required to act as a hostess and participate in genteel society.

The crucial first step for any young genteel woman wishing to enter this society was the 'debut'.

•

In June 1905, 'Miss Mabel Kelly' was pictured in Melbourne's *Punch* magazine wearing a fashionable dress of chiffon and lace. There it was announced that during a dance given at Montalto the young Miss Kelly had made her societal 'debut'—a formal introduction to 'society' that was deemed a necessity for girls of her class.[1] A remnant of British aristocratic ritual, debuts were originally designed to present the daughters of the gentility to court in Britain so they could attend social events and announce their availability for marriage. In Australia, the 'coming out' process was less formal, and genteel girls generally made their debuts at a ball or a dance from around the age of seventeen or eighteen. Yet the debut continued to hold significance for some Australian girls' social standing, acting as a marker of young adulthood; indeed, the ritual has continued into the twenty-first century. As one social commentator noted in the early twentieth century, 'the advent into society marks the fact that the girl had reached years of discretion. Her school days are over, and she is old enough to take upon herself the responsibilities of life.'[2]

Following this milestone, Mab attended innumerable 'at-homes', dances, balls, tea parties and charity events, hosted by some of Melbourne's wealthiest socialites. In the winter of 1905 she was a noted guest at a series of events including an extravagant 'At Home' in Toorak held by Mrs Wesley Hall, the wife of a well-known Victorian philanthropist, and a charity ball held by leading Victorian philanthropist Janet, Lady Clarke at the Prahran Town Hall.[3] Images and descriptions of girls attending social occasions filled the 'women's sections' of Melbourne's magazines and periodicals, where the girls were described as stylishly dressed in various shades of chiffon, silk and lace, products of

MISS MABEL KELLY,
Daughter of Mr. George C. Kelly, who made her
debut at the dance given at "Montalto,"
Toorak, 19th May.
Photo by Vandyck.

'Miss Mabel Kelly' makes her debut, *Punch*, 1 June 1905.

the flourishing importation of luxurious fabrics into Australia's wealthiest metropole.

The social practice of being 'at home', in which genteel women received visitors at certain advertised hours for parties, dances and small gatherings, was another British import. By the early twentieth century, however, at-homes could refer to a reception or concert held in a private home, a club or a hotel. Mab hosted several at-home events at Montalto and in other semi-public settings, entertaining and socialising with other young ladies and men. In November 1905 she hosted a 'particularly enjoyable' tea party at Montalto. Wearing a 'lettuce green spotted crepe de chine', she received her guests at the entrance to the drawing room, which was filled with vibrant floral decorations, 'dainty refreshments' and musical entertainment.[4] These social occasions necessitated the maintenance of the elaborate social customs and standards associated with being a graceful hostess and a well-mannered guest—skills that Mab would exercise throughout her life.

FROM MONTALTO
TO MIEGUNYAH

Marriage required that Mab shed her role as dilettante and step into a new position as wife, hostess and lady of the house. Miegunyah was the setting for this transition. The property had been named in the nineteenth century, most likely from an appropriation of the Aboriginal word *gunyah*, meaning 'home' or 'dwelling' in the Dharuk (Dharug) language of Sydney.[5] During the early twentieth century, Toorak remained a small and extremely affluent locality, occupied by the city's 'old money' and nouveau riche. Elaborate Italianate mansions built during the boom of the 1880s made up the bulk of the private residences, while shops and mercantile banks, churches and several private schools dotted the neighbourhood, all comprising a thriving community.

While Miegunyah has some Italianate elements, its design is unique and today it stands out in the sea of sleek contemporary mansions and residences

Opposite, Mab reading newspaper in Miegunyah garden, April 1917.
Following spread, Miegunyah, October 1933.

built in the Tudor Revival, neo-Georgian and neoclassical styles. Its distinctive appearance is a testament to the Grimwades' innovative and eccentric tastes. The property was both a reflection of their passions and interests and the nexus for their social and family life. They employed some of the best architects in Victoria to expand and alter Miegunyah, which was transformed from a modest colonial structure into an impressive two-storey, twelve-roomed mansion. From the time of Mab and Russell's arrival in 1911 over the following five decades, the property underwent a succession of ambitious alterations reflecting its owners' changing interests and tastes.

The most substantial changes occurred in 1920–21 and 1933–34. The Arts and Crafts–style alterations made in the 1920s, including the addition of a baronial-style panelled hall, a chamfered fireplace, and the gallery housing the Grimwades' print collection, have been attributed by Miles Lewis to one of the leading Melbourne architects associated with this movement, Harold Desbrowe-Annear.[6] In the 1930s, Stephenson and Meldrum, a prominent architectural firm in Melbourne, made a series of alterations, including on the north-eastern corner of the building a new drawing room fitted with windows rising up the wall and enclosed by French shutters. Imposing twin columns now stretched from terrace to roof on the garden side of the building, adding a note of grandeur. Stained-glass windows overlooked the extensive grounds; the grounds were also altered and expanded over time.

Mab and Russell's interest in horticulture and botany found expression in the Miegunyah garden, which served both a functional and a decorative purpose. It included a eucalypt arboretum, a productive kitchen garden, elaborate rose beds, stretches of plane trees and a pond with a bronze statue. Like the house, the garden is the work of some of the best landscape architects in Australia, including Edna Walling, Ellis Stones, EF Cook and John Stevens.

While the design of Miegunyah and its grounds is associated with Russell's creative vision, Mab was evidently involved in shaping the interior of the home; its aesthetic certainly reflected her taste for classic design and her preference for pinks and florals and warm, inviting and comfortable spaces. Miegunyah was the showcase for the Grimwades' substantial collection of

Opposite, Mab on the steps of Miegunyah with a young relative, April 1918.
Following pages, Miegunyah interior, November 1931.

furniture, art, botanical specimens, texts and Australiana. The interiors evoked a sense of nostalgia and evinced artistic innovation and skill, with furnishings including seventeenth- and eighteenth-century oak pieces collected by the Grimwades on overseas trips and also pieces crafted by Russell himself. Richly patterned Persian rugs covered the timber floors; walls were hung with artworks by some of the most influential contemporary and classical artists. In 1929, one commentator described Miegunyah's interior as 'some picture of the past, with its medieval-panelled hall and ... gallery, while ancient fire irons gleam from the immense hearth, and antique-brass plates and vessels shine like flame against the dark wood'.[7] Despite its stylistic preoccupation with the European past, Miegunyah was also a shrine to Australiana, with pride of place given to a stained-glass window depicting Captain Cook's *Endeavour*, designed by artist and friend of the Grimwades Daryl Lindsay.

At Miegunyah, Mab was responsible for overseeing a contingent of indoor and outdoor staff. Her childhood home would certainly have habituated her to life in a spacious mansion requiring considerable upkeep. Indeed, Camilla Kelly reflected that over time Mab 'became used to organising the staff—chauffeur and cook and another woman and gardeners—and expected obedience'.[8] The many bills and receipts left in Mab's archive from butchers, bakers, fishmongers, poulterers, fruiterers, florists, tobacco merchants and pharmacists hint at the daily administrative labour it took to manage the household.

In addition to this domestic labour, Mab was the orchestrator of all social events held in the public rooms at Miegunyah. According to John Poynter, she was more interested in socialising than her husband was, organising race meetings, official receptions, formal farewells and large functions that she persuaded Russell to attend.[9] During the interwar period she hosted several notable cocktail parties, receptions and dances at Miegunyah that made their way into the social pages. Guests were reported as enjoying extravagant flower arrangements and the hum of orchestral music, while expensive gowns and exclusive guest lists were noted, among them Australia's vice-regals, titans of industry, sportspeople and artists. On one occasion in spring 1937, Miegunyah's

Opposite, Miegunyah interior.
Following spread, Mab in motor car at Miegunyah
holding a Scottie dog, January 1916.

doors and grounds were opened to 500 guests for an 'After the races party'.[10] During such formal events, Mab's role as hostess included tasks defined in Edwardian etiquette manuals. She would have carefully selected the decor, including flower arrangements, and musical entertainment as well as the food menu, and, if it was a formal dinner, organised the seating arrangements and even the conversation topics in some cases.

In addition to being a productive space for socialising, networking and fundraising, Miegunyah was a source of comfort and enjoyment for Mab. Images of her in the house and garden show her joyful and relaxed, reading, embroidering, playing bridge, riding in new motor cars, spending time with her Scottish terriers and entertaining her nieces and nephews. Nieces and nephews were frequent visitors at Miegunyah, where they were doted upon by their affectionate Aunt Mab. Camilla Kelly recalled that 'when I stayed with her I always felt welcome & we often went to 1st nights of opera or ballet or some other interesting exhibition. She was very interested in all these things & loved dressing up for them in lovely clothes & jewellery.'[11]

•

While Miegunyah provided a home base for the Grimwades' busy social life in the city, the couple also spent much time exploring rural Victoria and visiting family and friends across the country. In 1920 they acquired a 100-acre (40-hectare) property at Baxter, near Frankston on the Mornington Peninsula, as the site for a country home. The tradition of keeping a second property in the country was a feature of middle- and upper-class living from the mid nineteenth century onward. The Mornington Peninsula became a popular holiday destination in the 1860s, providing a seaside escape from the city's intense summer heat; by the 1920s, many of Melbourne's affluent families owned holiday homes along the coast and further inland.

Harold Desbrowe-Annear was hired in the 1920s to design a two-storey Arts and Crafts–style house on the Grimwades' new property.[12] The design is unconventional, with no corridors and three wings extending from a central staircase. Stained timber was used for most of the interiors, and an elevated water tank is housed in a small timbered tower that rises from the centre of the

Opposite, Mab with dog at Miegunyah, June 1935.

41

Above, Panoramic view of Westerfield, April 1930.
Following spread, Mab with Daryl and
Joan Lindsay at Westerfield, December 1925.

cement-tile roof. The building was finished quickly, and the Grimwades spent their first Christmas at the newly named Westerfield in 1924.

Country properties were not simply rural escapes from city life: they were often spaces for work, even industry. Westerfield became both a beautiful and a productive site. The grounds included an area of natural bushland, a terraced lawn, a garden and pergola, an orchard, a vegetable garden and a timber windmill to generate electricity for the house. Russell populated the vast acreage with around fifty species of gum, together with lavender, roses and geraniums, from which he extracted natural oils.

Westerfield also provided another venue for entertaining guests and hosting relatives, becoming a popular destination for the honeymoons of younger family members. It was here that Mab and Russell formed a friendship with Daryl and Joan Lindsay, who lived at Mulberry Hill, 1.6 kilometres from Westerfield. Daryl was an artist from the famous Lindsay family and Joan the author of the novel *Picnic at Hanging Rock,* and the four shared an interest in art and Australiana that sustained a lifelong friendship. Mab took great pleasure spending time in Westerfield's lush grounds, and images abound of her enjoying the country air with various family members and friends. She also visited rural friends and family frequently, participating in country social life and enjoying regional race meets.

When Mab returned to the city, she maintained a busy social calendar, belonging to and patronising social, charitable, civic and cultural institutions. The social pages regularly noted her attendance—and gowns—at various dances, race meetings, garden receptions, charity balls, gallery openings, polo tournaments, mayoral dinners, and receptions for international dignitaries. She spent time at the centre of the city, socialising with other genteel women at the Lyceum and Alexandra clubs, two of the most prestigious private women's clubs in Victoria.

From the late nineteenth century, women's clubs were part of the renegotiation of public and private spheres; they were used for dining, taking tea, staging events and finding refuge in the heart of a city. At the Lyceum and Alexandra clubs, Mab mingled with members of Melbourne's cultural and social elite, including leading Victorian philanthropist Elisabeth Murdoch and principal commandant of the Australian Red Cross Alice Creswick, who was familiar with Mab through her work with the Free Kindergarten Union. The networks created at these women's clubs both reflected and fostered

25 · 2 · 35

Above, Mab embroidering at Miegunyah, February 1935.
Following spread, Mab with Scottish terrier at Westerfield, c. 1930.

the members' busy social lives and facilitated fundraising opportunities for their numerous charitable causes. Indeed, Mab's name appeared alongside Creswick's and Murdoch's in the guest lists of several formal charitable events throughout the first half of the twentieth century.[13]

The various societies and institutions with which Mab associated indicate political sympathies that combine conservative nationalism with appreciation of imperial ties. Her desire to conserve and protect Australian landscapes, culture and heritage is evident in her membership of the National Trust of Australia, the Native Plants Preservation Society of Victoria and the National Gallery Society. Although she was not outwardly political, Mab's subscription to the Liberal and Country Party and support of the Victoria League for Commonwealth Friendship—a charitable organisation supporting the preservation of ties among Commonwealth countries—indicate her political leanings and imperial loyalties.

Her interests often became investments in the future of Australian culture: a passion for art collection encouraged her support of the creative arts in Victoria. She was a member of the Arts and Crafts Society and the Victorian Artists' Society, a regular correspondent of and donor to the National Gallery of Victoria, and a member of the Little Theatre Guild, the Australian Elizabethan Theatre Trust and the Australian Ballet Company. As Lady Grimwade, she was invited to the opening nights of the National Theatre's ballet season and to fine art exhibitions, Shakespeare productions and Italian operas. Her patronage of such cultural institutions demonstrates her willingness to transpose elements of British 'high culture' to Victoria, and her determination to participate in the development of a unique and flourishing Victorian society.

•

From her debut at age eighteen, Mab entered a social landscape populated by Australia's upper class and shaped by customs and values that prescribed certain responsibilities for women. It was a world dominated by married genteel women, but although they performed their duties as diligent wives and sophisticated hostesses, Mab and her social circle were not bound by the domestic sphere. Their busy social lives challenged boundaries between the 'public'

Opposite, Mab and Russell at Westerfield, January 1928
Following spread, Mab and companion at Westerfield, April 1930

and 'private' worlds. At-homes could provide opportunities for both social-ising and networking; elaborate parties were crucial avenues for fundraising and the development of cultural capital. Miegunyah and Westerfield provided ample ground for Mab to cultivate and maintain her and Russell's social and familial relationships.

While she enjoyed the logistics and pageantry of large social events, Mab's social life was entwined with her philanthropic work, and the various societies she patronised reflect a concern with preserving Australia's natural and cultural landscapes. Miegunyah and Westerfield were emblems of this urge to conserve and construct Victorian culture at home. The house, grounds and interiors of Miegunyah bridged past, present and future: today, the property remains a monument to Australian life in the wake of Federation and the Great War, and central to the Grimwades' legacy.

Chapter 3.
ABROAD

'we drove into The Taj Mahal &
all that has been said of it is true.
When you get the first glimpse
of it framed in the huge red
stone gateway you simply gasp.'

MAB GRIMWADE 1921

On 5 February 1921 Mab and Russell embarked on P&O's SS *Naldera*, a newly
built steam liner recently dispatched to Australia from London. In his and
Mab's daybook, Russell noted that the large passenger ship 'dawdled with a
record number of passengers through southern waters'.[1] The liner was bound
for the port of Colombo in Ceylon (Sri Lanka), where the Grimwades would
take a six-week tour on their way to Europe.

In the early twentieth century, Mab and Russell were two of thousands
of Australians who were travelling overseas at unprecedented rates. Some
went for work or to be with their family, others were forced across borders. The
Grimwades travelled for pleasure, maintaining an itinerant and luxurious lifestyle and acting the tourist at various ports and towns across the world. From
1920 to 1927, they traversed the Indian and Atlantic oceans, visiting the peripheries and centre of the British Empire and venturing into the New World.

The advent of steam shipping and the opening of the Suez Canal in the
mid nineteenth century revolutionised international travel, compressing time
and space by lessening the duration and improving the quality of journeys.
Large steam liners could accommodate up to 2000 passengers divided into
three classes. In the new twentieth-century steamers, first-class passengers like
the Grimwades occupied the ship's upper deck and could expect berths that

Opposite, Mab with friends Lorna and Dennis
Sargood on the banks of the Loire, November 1921.
Following spread, Mab winning a deck quoits
competition on the RMS *Niagara*, July 1923.

were designed as floating microcosms of genteel homes, grand saloons filled with ornate furniture and large palm trees, comfortable sleeping quarters fitted with Egyptian-cotton sheets, and chef-prepared meals offered nightly. New steamers also provided more space for recreation, and the addition of promenade and boat decks allowed sunbathing and the playing of deck games such as quoits, shuttlecock, cricket and badminton. Indoors, passengers played bridge and entertainment was offered in the form of dances, concerts and theatrical performances.

The expansion of steamship routes from Australia across the globe in the early twentieth century coincided with the growth of Australian travel writing. Mab and Russell shared a daybook chronicling their joint travels, and after Russell's death Mab continued documenting her daily movements on many of her trips. Travel diaries were a common way for Australians to record their experiences and fashion their identities when overseas. People who usually would not write felt obliged to note their observations, preserving their encounters and adventures for themselves or a wider audience.

As with most travel diaries, Mab's entries detail both the mundane and the extraordinary. While much of her writing summarises the logistics of travel, the weather and the various lunches, hotels and shopping trips undertaken, her more thoughtful observations show a preoccupation with aesthetics: she describes in great detail the architectural character of each city she visits, and marvels at the diverse natural landscapes she encounters. While many female travellers during this period crossed borders in search of fresh identities, creative inspiration or opportunities for education and work, Mab travelled in search of enjoyment, new experiences and knowledge, and artworks and antiques to add to the Grimwades' collection. In her diary entries, she represents herself as a sophisticated tourist, an arbiter of taste, a subject of Empire and, above all, an 'Australian abroad'.

The SS *Naldera* took around sixteen days to cross the Indian Ocean and the Laccadive Sea before docking at the bustling port of Colombo, the entrepôt for global trade with the Indian subcontinent and at that time the seventh-biggest port in the world. The Grimwades' luggage was carried onto the wharf, where they were welcomed by a local man named Missa Prema who entered the couple's service 'at once'.

In the 1920s, British imperial power in India and Ceylon was challenged by nationalist sects, yet the country remained under British hegemony, and wealthy Australian tourists were afforded all the privileges of the 'ruling' caste. An image of Mab in Darjeeling, seated happily in a rickshaw pulled by four Indian men, epitomises the way the Grimwades experienced India and Ceylon as members of this ruling elite. As Australians they would have felt entitled to such a status in British colonies. Indeed, their diary entries are imbued with language and perspectives that reflect the pervasive colonial discourse of self and 'other' that characterised much of Australian travel writing during the 'Age of Empire'.

As Australian travellers with imperial networks and disposable income, they could observe the artefacts of ancient and medieval India while enjoying the comforts and pleasures of genteel life. Mab and Russell explored bazaars, temples, mosques and ruins while staying in grand hotels, visiting botanical gardens, playing golf and eating tiffin. Mab's diary entries suggest an energetic and curious traveller who was struck by the contrast between India's sublime beauty and its widespread poverty. She carefully describes the imposing marble and sandstone palaces of Agra, and recalls a profound experience witnessing the Taj Mahal at sunset:

> ... we drove into The Taj Mahal & all that has been said of it is true. When you get the first glimpse of it framed in the huge red stone gateway you simply gasp ... You visit the place with great curiosity & excitement ... prepared to be disappointed but I have never heard of or could imagine anyone being once they have seen it. It seems to stir you up & appeal to you in the most tender way.

During the Grimwades' tour, Mab's romantic expectations of the Indian subcontinent were tempered by reality, and many of her diary entries note the inconveniences of travel throughout the country and the inadequate service of their local employees. She writes of a 'long and tedious and filthy' train journey from Calcutta to Darjeeling, and complains about the 'unbearable' Delhi heat and various instances of misplaced luggage and lost hotel bookings. When their party finally reaches Marseilles after a two-week ship ride, Mab expresses the greatest relief to be welcomed into the 'beautiful and luxurious rooms' of the Hôtel de Louvre.

Following spread, Mab seated on a rickshaw in Darjeeling, March 1921.

Many Australians were drawn to Europe's cultural capital during the interwar period: France represented the forefront of artistic endeavour and evoked a sense of romance and enchantment. While Paris was the world's centre for art, the south of France was home to some of the country's most beautiful natural landscapes, its fields of lavender and picturesque seaside towns captured by French impressionists in the nineteenth century. From Marseilles, Mab and Russell were driven in a Delaunay-Belleville motor car through Provence, where they visited the medieval ruins at Baux, and Roman remains at Arles and Nîmes. On their route, Mab noted the 'wonderfully green & fresh' countryside, with 'judas tree & lilac in full bloom'. They lunched at various chateaux, stayed at luxury hotels and went shopping for Cartier antiques. The Belleville took them through to Valence, Grenoble and Lyon, ending the tour in Paris.

In the northern summer, Mab and Russell made their pilgrimage to the imperial metropolis, staying at a friend's apartment in London and periodically visiting Scotland and the west of England. For many Australians in the early twentieth century, Britain was still the 'centre of the world', the locus of a shared historical and cultural heritage and the stimulus for an emotional connection to an imagined past. The Grimwades would have felt a sense of belonging in Britain, compounded by the strength of their network of relatives and friends across the country. A photograph of Mab taken in London during this trip, wearing a classic straight-cut lace and sheer cotton dress appropriate for a 'royal occasion', hints at the social circles the Grimwades frequented while visiting the United Kingdom.

By November the Grimwades were back in France, joined by some Australian friends for a tour of the battlefields of Flanders and the Loire Valley. Mab was impressed by the sight of the Loire Valley in the autumn, and enjoyed visiting the chateaux, castles and medieval towns dotting the countryside:

> Crossing the Loire you go all through rural country the Autumn colouring being wonderful. The absence of hedges & fences is most noticeable after Eng. & also the flatness. You then come to the Park of Chambord wh. is the largest in France wh. leads to the enormous Castle built by Francis I. It is a mass of towers & turrets … It really is a wonderful piece of work.

Opposite, Portrait of Mab in London, July 1921.

Above, Mab and others observing the eclipse
in Coronado, California, September 1923.
Opposite, Château de Chambord, November 1921.

After ten months abroad, Mab and Russell returned to Australia. They were laden with expensive souvenirs and stories of their journey from the margins to the heart of the British Empire, and through the romantic French countryside.

•

Just two years later, in 1923, Mab and Russell left Sydney for Auckland on the SS *Niagara*, stopping over for a few days of golf and a visit to the Botanic Gardens before embarking on a 'Great American Adventure'.[2] Their American sojourn was spent pursuing their interests in golf, motoring, botany, astronomy and collecting. Arriving in Honolulu, they visited a pineapple-canning factory where Mab witnessed the height of American industrial efficiency:

> The Pineapple Canning Factory [was] a most wonderful & interesting sight, where you saw all the pineapples in the world I shd [sic] think. They canned 11,000 tons of fruit a day. Over 2000 hands all looking smart & clean, the women in white caps & aprons & rubber clothese [sic].

Mab was impressed by Honolulu's 'beautifully laid out' urban landscape and diverse plant life, noting the 'gay and artistic' hibiscus-hedge- and olean-der-lined streets, and the translucent pastels and lush greens of the famous Windward Coast, including 'tropical things then roses, gladioli, asters'.

British Columbia was next, and in Victoria, Mab and Russell visited the observatory, enjoying a tour from the chief astronomer, Dr Harry Plaskett, before being 'rudely disturbed by American rubbernecks'. The golf links in British Columbia were difficult yet 'charming', and the couple were 'very taken with a revolving sprinkler there': Russell promptly ordered four.

From Vancouver they travelled southwards to Seattle, Portland and, finally, San Francisco. Mab admired the 'beautiful scenery and wonder-ful rivers' of the west coast, and at each destination the voyagers were met with perfect weather and supreme golfing conditions. They spent a week in San Francisco, where they lunched with the president of the University of California and his wife. After visiting another observatory on the summit of Mount Hamilton in San Jose, Mab spent the day shopping and then embarked with Russell on an evening journey to Yosemite Valley.

The trip to Yosemite Valley proved less than successful. They endured a crowded, hot and uncomfortable train ride to Yosemite Lodge, arriving 'very dirty and exhausted'. The grandeur of the valley, with its stretches of hillside covered in giant redwoods and sequoias giving way to 900-metre mountain rocks, provided some respite for Mab. But she was dismayed by the 'swarms of people' at the lodge, where she witnessed 'most awful sights of women in knickers and breeches with silk stockings & high-heeled shoes, painted faces—much curled hair—rigs for hiking ... swimming baths—open air dancing, concerts etc. rather resembling Luna Park'. Russell too recoiled at the sight of 'millions of citizens in all styles of the most repugnant garb ... defiling the quietude of the valley floor with their very presence and appearance'. These rather comical observations reflect the Grimwades' resistance to mass tourism, certain aspects of modernity, and what they would have seen as 'improper' behaviour. They were accustomed to travelling in style and preferred quiet, open spaces, tidy and orderly towns, and comfortable hotels.

In late August the couple headed southwards towards Coronado, near San Diego, to witness an eclipse. Along the way they stopped to play golf, drove over the Monterey Peninsula and followed the Pacific Coast Highway through Santa Barbara to Los Angeles. In LA they stayed at a hotel in Beverly Hills, socialising with artistic and well-connected friends. Through such connections, Mab and Russell were invited to visit the set of *The Thief of Baghdad*, starring the silent film 'sensation' Douglas Fairbanks. Mab was titillated by the visit, and after meeting Fairbanks himself proclaimed him to be 'the most marvellous man', commending him for his ingenuity and natural charm. Pages of her diary were dedicated to describing their tour of the Pickford–Fairbanks Studios:

> The attention to every detail is astounding. They take 4 films one for themselves one for the States one for England & Europe & two others for Asia & Australia. We then went all round the studio & saw all the different settings which are mostly destroyed as soon as the picture is finished, but am glad to say some of Robin Hood with its castle drawbridge were still left—absolutely correct in every detail—they had 2 men working for 6 months in the British Museum collecting data. They have artists, literary men, scientists & every branch on the

Following pages, Mab on donkey-back in Egypt, February 1927.

Above, Mab on the Amalfi Coast, March 1927.
Opposite, Mab sightseeing in Cairo, Egypt, February 1927.

staff ... The costume room was a revelation with his costumes nearly all made in beautiful silk materials and every detail thought of—all the supers take their costumes back each night—the stars keep theirs in their dressing rooms ...The wig makers draftsmen & every thing in the place—one of the most entertaining & interesting tours—only wish it had been cooler.

This was the form of modernity that excited Mab—one that combined artistic innovation with large-scale production. The rest of the trip was relatively anticlimactic after witnessing Hollywood on the brink of its 'golden age': Coronado was disappointing, and the eclipse was obscured by poor weather. On 21 September Mab and Russell sailed home in the RMS *Tahiti*, arriving in Melbourne in mid-October.

•

The couple took their third overseas trip in six years towards the end of 1926, travelling for almost eleven months through Egypt, Europe and England. Beginning in Port Said and ending in Naples, this trip was dominated by visits to cultural institutions and the collection of art and antiques. The SS *Oronsay* arrived at Port Said, a cosmopolitan hub of Empire, global trade and tourism, in January 1927. From there, the Grimwades embarked on a tour of Egypt, travelling up the Nile and stopping to ride on donkey-back to visit tombs, temples and pyramids. Just as in India, they travelled as privileged citizens of Empire, freely traversing the British-occupied territory equipped with an interpreter and manservants. As John Poynter writes of their trip there, 'it was the classical Egyptian excursion in the area of British predominance, with lunch at the Residency, drinks and meals at Shepheard's Hotel, and golf at the Gizerah [Gezira] Sporting Club'.[3] In the company of an exclusive network of wealthy British and Australian expatriates, the Grimwades toured the Cairo Museum, the remains of the Nile temples and the great temple of Amon at Karnak, travelling beyond to Second Cataract and back to Cairo.

The couple then sailed to Gibraltar via Naples, crossing to Tangier before boarding the *Arcadian* for a Mediterranean cruise. They stopped at various ports in the Mediterranean; a highlight was the Palazzo Montalto in Sicily, although the pleasure of the voyage was tainted by crowded ships and inadequate tour guides. On return to Gibraltar, they were met by a chauffeur in a Crossley car to take them across southern Spain. In Granada, Mab and Russell revelled in the splendid architecture and formal gardens of the Alhambra, and were delighted by the art galleries in Seville and Madrid and the famous mosque at Córdoba. From Spain, they travelled north to Paris and Holland in search of fine dining, haute couture, oak furniture and European masterpieces.

By the end of April Mab and Russell were once again in England, where they attempted to view another eclipse in Yorkshire. After a long stretch in the United Kingdom, they took the Orient Express to Munich, Vienna and Hungary, where they had private tours of various palaces and galleries. Italy was the final destination of their tour itinerary; in Venice, they visited the Murano glass factory and enjoyed the customary gondola rides along winding canals and the passing parade in the Piazza San Marco, while Florence, Rome and Naples provided more opportunities for the collection of art and antiques.

Mab and Russell returned home with an enriched understanding and appreciation for European art, and an expanded private collection to fill the rooms of Miegunyah. Photographs reveal that they continued to travel throughout the 1930s, returning to the United Kingdom, the United States and Europe, and exploring East Asia and South Africa.

•

In the 1950s and 1960s the boom of commercial air travel extended the horizon for international movement. This was the 'Golden Age of Air Travel', with the introduction of the jet aircraft heralding a new era of fast and efficient overseas journeys that allowed the Grimwades to travel more frequently and for shorter periods of time. New aircraft were fitted with spacious cabins, modern amenities and tastefully decorated lounges, and offered premium cuisine.

In 1953, Mab and Russell set off on a ten-week 'holiday cruise' to China and Japan, despite Russell having suffered a severe heart attack earlier in the year. In the 1950s direct flights could be taken from Melbourne to former imperial capitals across Asia, and the Grimwades joined a wave of Australian tourists drawn to East Asia in the postwar period. Australian magazines advertised Japan's luxurious 'cherry blossom cruises'; in contrast, travel to the

Following spread, Mab 'under the olives', unknown location, April 1927.

People's Republic of China after the communist revolution and, later, during the Cultural Revolution proved difficult for international visitors.[4]

Mab and Russell passed through other ports in East Asia, including Kure, Yokohama and Nagoya in Japan. According to an interview with Mab in *The Age*, this was her second visit to East Asia after her first seventeen years earlier, and 'the rapid growth of the population in ... Japan had been a revelation'.[5] She witnessed the explosion of commercial enterprise in Japan, and her observations echo the general portrayal of Japan by the West during this time as a country unique in its mixture of 'oriental' tradition and futuristic technology. She expressed amazement at the 'way in which the people worked ... They were most industrious ... and were turning out technical goods—such as cameras and field glasses—with great efficiency.'[6]

Two years later, Mab and Russell were back in London for six weeks on what would be their last overseas trip together, lured by the prospect of purchasing what would become the crown jewel of their Australiana collection, William Strutt's *Bushrangers* (1852). They travelled home on an ocean liner, the SS *Orcades*, via the Panama Canal. Russell described the tumultuous journey back to Australia in a letter to a friend:

> Our trip was none too easy ... I fell ill with a series of heart attacks which caused Mab great concern, and to spare her we did the very wise thing of asking Clive Fitts [the Grimwades' doctor] to come over from Sydney to accept responsibility for getting me to Melbourne. Clive was splendid and gave Mab a relief from anxiety that she had not experienced in several weeks.[7]

The palpable sense of anxiety described by Russell here intimates Mab's devotion to her husband. Russell Grimwade died on 2 November 1955 at the age of seventy-six. It is hard to imagine and impossible to articulate the profound grief Mab would have felt at losing her closest companion of more than forty years. Over time, she adjusted to life without him and continued to travel with friends, although she did so less frequently.

•

Mab with friends in Blinda, Algeria, March 1927.

In April 1957 Mab was bound for Europe by way of Honolulu and Vancouver, where she took a 'most exciting and thrilling flight over the snow covered Rockies [in] Alberta'.[8] She was accompanied on her journey by a series of friends, most of whom she mentions only by first or last name. Mab's focus for this sojourn was enriching her knowledge of historical and contemporary European art. Arriving in Amsterdam and travelling through Holland, she immersed herself in that country's cultural and artistic institutions, spending most of her time gazing at the familiar artworks of the great masters: 'After lunch Mauritshuis Picture Gallery—The Anatomy Lecture by Rembrandt—Vermeers—Cranach—Flemish Primitives—Holbein'. At the Municipal Museum in Leiden, she perused its collection of post-impressionists: Van Gogh, Monet, Toulouse-Lautrec and Degas.

She spent the following months on a tour of Italy, travelling southwards from Isola Madre, an island in the Isole Borromee archipelago in Lake Maggiore in northern Italy, through Milan and then to Venice by way of Verona and Padua, ending with a few days in Florence and Rome. Her diary entries bear the usual descriptions of grand hotels and villas, impressive formal gardens, towering cathedrals, and damask-lined galleries of Renaissance and Baroque paintings. She favours the 'primitives'—paintings of the Renaissance period—and searches for the Italian masters at each stop on the tour: she sees Leonardo da Vinci's *The Last Supper* in Milan, Botticelli, Raphael and Michelangelo in Florence, and Tiepolo, Tintoretto and Bellini in Venice. In Rome she purchases 'hand woven tapestries', tours the Colosseum and Forum, strolls through the Villa Medici gardens, and wonders how Michelangelo had painted the Sistine Chapel 'while lying on his back'.

The last documented part of the journey was in Paris, a familiar city for the well-travelled Mab. Although now rivalled by New York, it remained the world's artistic centre for many in the 1950s, and naturally the Louvre was Mab's first port of call. Here she 'longed to dally into the Primitives' but found the French impressionists instead: 'lost my heart to 2 Renoirs & some Corots'. After unsuccessfully seeking a dose of modern art at the Académie Moderne and the Orangerie, she and her party lunched at the Australian embassy with

Opposite, Mab in private gardens with
companion in Kyoto, March 1936.
Following spread, Mab reclining by a motor car with
friends and stray dogs in Bolton, England, March 1932.

several expatriates and the consul general of Denmark. She flew home via Honolulu in October on the *Southern Breeze* aircraft, her appetite for European art well and truly satiated.

Three years later, in September 1960, Mab flew to the United States for a short visit, pursuing an interest in that country's colonial history and heritage. This trip was meticulously organised and documented, each portion of the day accounted for in a travel itinerary written by an assistant.[9] While in Farmington, Connecticut, Mab enjoyed luncheons and dinners with various dignitaries, artists, writers and titans of industry.[10] Over the course of a few days, she dined with Corinne Aslop Cole (née Douglas-Robinson), niece of Theodore Roosevelt; the president of the New York Botanical Garden; and the well-known author Grace Flandrau. She documented her travels through photographs of buildings and landscapes, and collected booklets, tourist brochures and postcards as souvenirs. Extending her expertise in heritage, she took a short course on 'Historic Housekeeping' in Cooperstown, New York as a representative of the National Trust of Australia.[11] She immersed herself in the historical landscapes of colonial America, visiting various historic homes and collecting their stories. An eight-day trip to the centre of the American south proved busy and informative. In Arkansas's capital, Little Rock, Mab visited the Territorial Capitol Restoration buildings and the Fine Art Gallery, met with local dignitaries and business owners, watched a university football game, and attended Presbyterian services. She departed Arkansas via an American Airlines flight, returning home from what would be her last international journey.

•

Mab enjoyed both the transience of travel and the permanence of home. While her international sojourns speak to the broader phenomenon of 'Australians abroad' during the first half of the twentieth century, Mab's particular experience of travel was shaped by her class and status. Travel informed her identity as a distinguished tourist, a global consumer, a subject of the British Empire and an Australian. Leaving Australia afforded her the joy of extending her amateur expertise in art, architecture and botany. As she encountered new cultures and landscapes she maintained the lifestyle she was accustomed to, seeking the comforts and pursuits of home in golfing, motoring, lavish accommodation and a community of wealthy expatriates and friends.

Chapter 4.

PHILANTHROPY AND CHARITY WORK

'Model Hats Displayed', *The Age*, July 1951.

The Herald commended Mab for the 'original idea', which included competitions for the 'smallest dog; the most bandy-legged dog; dog with the best tricks; the dog with the most sympathetic eyes'

THE HERALD 1941

On a Sunday evening in July 1951, Miegunyah's reception rooms were packed with Melbourne's *haute monde,* eager to enjoy Lady Grimwade's 'hat parade'. The event displayed Sydney society milliner Stella Fraenkel's finest hats and headdresses in aid of the Isabel Henderson Kindergarten.

Fraenkel was one of the most prestigious milliners in Australia during the 1950s, and her hats were highly sought after among Sydney and Melbourne society women. Miegunyah's interior was transformed into a 'miniature Royal Ascot enclosure' and filled with well-known Melbourne women who modelled extravagant headdresses, posing as mannequins in mirror frames set in a wall covered in mushroom velvet curtains.[1] Dozens of tickets were sold, and guests included stars of the stage Evelyn Laye and her husband, Frank Lawton, and star jockey Jack Purtell. The parade's comical finale introduced Mab's Scottish terriers—Peggy, Susan and Judy—dressed in full regalia for a formal wedding.

In the social pages, the event was declared 'a success both financially and socially—and from a fashion point of view'.[2] Mab was its orchestrator, splitting her duties 'between behind-the-scenes organisation and the welcoming of her guests'.[3] The profits from the parade went to fund a new building for the Isabel Henderson Kindergarten in Fitzroy, of which Mab was president.

While Lady Grimwade's hat parade featured the latest styles in millinery, her fundraising methods evoked those of wealthy nineteenth-century women who belonged to ladies' benevolent societies. Such traditional philanthropic at-home exhibitions relied on a network of wealthy patrons wishing to advertise their moral virtue, enhance their social status and exchange charitable donations for entertainment. The continued existence of such events well into the twentieth century reveals the endurance of this tradition of women's philanthropy within elite social circles in Melbourne's wealthy southern suburbs. The Grimwades' Toorak estate was in constant use for fundraising events, providing scope for Mab's philanthropic energies, organisational skills and social prowess. But her philanthropic and charity work was not confined to fundraising events among Melbourne's upper class: she took an active role in various social and cultural causes that were important to her, giving both her time and money to support and develop many of Victoria's educational, social, civic and cultural institutions.

Mab grew up in a social class that saw philanthropy and charity work as a social expectation and a duty to those 'less fortunate'. This sense of *noblesse oblige* was inherited by Australia's social elite from the British aristocracy. However, the necessity of fulfilling social responsibilities assumed new meaning in the colonies, where financial endowments and government-funded public volunteer associations were central to the building of new communities.

Philanthropy played a pivotal role in creating Victorian society in the nineteenth and early twentieth centuries, with various cultural institutions and welfare societies established in colonial Victoria requiring patronage and volunteerism to develop. Informed by the nascent patriotism of the genteel class in early twentieth-century Melbourne, much of this early philanthropy charged itself with forging a vibrant Victorian culture and an 'egalitarian' nation. Social, philanthropic and charitable organisations emerged, born of a Christian and humanitarian concern for the social welfare of marginalised communities. State welfare programs were implemented in conjunction with both government-funded and private voluntary and charitable societies to instigate social change. The creation of the Australian welfare state after Federation in 1901 extended government social provisions to the public, including old age pensions and maternity allowances, yet philanthropy and voluntary charity remained an important sector of the Victorian economy throughout the twentieth century as a supplement to state provisions. This was an arena in which women played a crucial role.

While genteel women were expected to maintain social hierarchies primarily through their participation in the domestic sphere, philanthropy was encouraged as part of the structure of elite society. Historian Shirlee Swain notes that 'for women, the primary attraction to philanthropy was that it confirmed their gentility'.[4] For Mab and other elite women, affiliating with charitable institutions and fundraising organisations and giving generous donations also had other purposes. Such work enabled them to exercise an altruistic duty and help to shape the future of Victorian society; it also indicated social status, garnered a positive social reputation, and provided them with access to power that was otherwise denied them. During the late nineteenth and early twentieth centuries, while wealthy men set up formal trust funds and philanthropic foundations for cultural institutions, women's philanthropy often centred on social welfare and providing ameliorative relief for the 'less fortunate'.

Today, philanthropy and charity are viewed as distinct. Historian of volunteerism Melanie Oppenheimer contrasts charity, which involves a religious component, and philanthropy, which is 'based on broader humanitarian principles', while Barbara Lemon distinguishes between those philanthropists who 'serve others' from those who 'serve others *using money*'.[5] However, during Mab's lifetime these distinctions were less applicable, and the impulse to serve others often combined religious and humanitarian aims, and both practical and financial support.[6] Philanthropy at that time could have referred to all aspects of charity and charitable services, including leagues, volunteerism and not-for-profit organisations. Mab's philanthropy took the form of financial assistance and patronage, volunteer work, fundraising campaigns and organisational leadership. Her philanthropy combined a dedication to expanding the arts and education, to social welfare and to the environment. Importantly, her philanthropic work was not solely backed by her husband's wealth: she was an innovative fundraiser and often put her own money towards the causes she supported. She used her wealth and influence to advance these causes, being aware of the social prestige her name offered.

•

Wealthy female philanthropists in the first half of the twentieth century often came from affluent Melbourne neighbourhoods such as Toorak, South Yarra, Armadale and Malvern. They were most often members of the city's premier private women's clubs, the Lyceum and the Alexandra. A glimpse of the social calendars of some of Melbourne's elite women during this period would reveal a string of at-homes and elaborate parties and events—all widely accepted avenues for fundraising among the upper class in Victoria. Society papers were furnished with accounts of fundraising balls, exhibitions and tea parties, including their prestigious guest lists and descriptions of elegant costumes and generous donations. Popular institutions and movements receiving support included the Free Kindergarten Union of Victoria, the Red Cross, the National Council of Women, benevolent societies, and various hospitals and organisations dedicated to wartime efforts and supporting returned servicemen.

In 1915, one year after World War I broke out, Mab organised a clothing and 'comforts' collection for the 4th Field Artillery Brigade prior to their embarkation for overseas service in Egypt. The collection included 'socks, shirts, comforter caps, scarfs, cigarettes', which Mab suggested would be 'more useful than pyjamas and such supplies issued by the Red Cross'.[7] Mab would have felt honour-bound to take on an active role in fundraising and organising on the home front. The Great War mobilised women of all classes who were eager to serve both the nation and Empire; they contributed to the war effort by volunteering for and donating to the premier wartime charities, including the Red Cross and the Australian Comforts Fund, along with organising fundraising drives and knitting and sewing campaigns, and practising thrift.

Mab supported the war effort during World War II, too, associating with the Australian Comforts Fund and the Red Cross from at least 1941. In that year, she hosted a meeting at Miegunyah to form an 'Australian Ballet Society' that would give regular seasons of ballet to raise money for the Red Cross Prisoners of War Fund.[8] She also participated in welfare programs for returned soldiers and soldiers on leave, including Royal Navy House, an institution that provided soldiers on leave with accommodation, meals and entertainment.[9] In 1961, she donated to the War Memorial Welfare Centre.

As working-class and middle-class women increasingly became part of the professionalised workforce from the late nineteenth century, elite women such as Mab cultivated their own forms of professionalism and expertise in their philanthropic roles. The coordination of large-scale fundraising events entailed an organisational skill set involving networking, running meetings, publicity campaigns and fundraising. If done well, this work could prove exceedingly successful in raising money for cultural institutions and charity organisations.

Mab developed this expertise over time, putting her social influence and organisational abilities to work developing and fundraising for various causes. She applied a personal touch to the events she organised at Miegunyah, which reflected her interests and hobbies. While the 'hat parade' at Miegunyah was inspired by her love of millinery, her interests in art, gardening and canines were manifested in numerous art shows and competitions, open gardens, and even a 'comical dog show'. Perhaps in an effort to create a reputation as an innovative fundraiser and host amid an endless array of tea parties and craft sales, Mab held the dog show on the Miegunyah grounds in 1931 to aid the Victorian Association of Braille Writers. Indeed, *The Herald* commended Mab for the 'original idea', which included competitions for the 'smallest dog; the most bandy-legged dog; dog with the best tricks; the dog with the most sympathetic eyes', judged by the Grimwades' friends Daryl Lindsay and Rupert Fanning.[10]

Fundraising events were not exclusively at-home affairs, and Mab helped to orchestrate several large-scale events for the University of Melbourne. From the 1950s, she took on the role of benefactor and committee member for various fundraising committees at the university. In October 1952 she was the president of the newly formed International House committee, tasked with raising funds for the furnishings and living quarters of the residential college that provided accommodation for overseas and Australian students. The committee comprised the wife of the vice-chancellor of the university, GW Paton, and several other influential Victorian women, including Lady Howe, Lady Medley and Lady McConnan. After some deliberation, they decided on an International House fete, to be held over two days in May 1953. Over the following months, Mab oversaw the securing of stallholders, volunteers, entertainers and a venue, and the advertising for the event. The fete was an organisational feat involving the work of 1000 students, 7000 volunteers and a dedicated executive committee. Held in the parking space between Union House and the colleges, it included around 200 stalls selling produce, baked goods, crafts, gardening requisites, flowers and children's clothing, as well as musical entertainment,

Following spread, 'Comical Dog Show' at Miegunyah, November 1931.

'Comical Dog Show' at Miegunyah, November 1931.

a pageant and a horticultural show. The fete was a great success, and Mab presented a cheque for £13,500 to the president of the International House fund in July 1953.[11] Two years later, she chaired the women's centenary committee of the Melbourne University Centenary Appeal, organising a hat pageant 'of beauty and history through the ages' held in Melba Hall.[12]

Such events demonstrate the vital role women's philanthropy and organising played in the infrastructural and cultural development of the University of Melbourne. Mab continued her support for the university through several generous donations and, later, the Miegunyah Fund and Bequests.

From the mid-twentieth century, Mab provided financial assistance to various organisations aiding the visually impaired, including the Victorian Association of Braille Writers and the Victorian Association for the Blind. In 1957, two years after Russell died, she gave a generous donation in aid of the Victorian ophthalmic surgeon Joseph Ringland Anderson's research into the study of the visually impaired. For this donation, she received a heartfelt letter from Helen Keller, a leading activist for people with disabilities in the first half of the twentieth century:

> Dear Lady Grimwade, Already I feel a precious bond of sympathy between you and me since I received a letter from Dr. Ringland Anderson telling of your splendid gift to the Institute for the Study of the Causes and Prevention of Blindness. You are among the champions of a true civilization that seeks to keep the light in all human eyes, and the joy and increased usefulness which shall flow from your noble deed will return to your heart filling it with sweetness. You are full of true courage, and I marvel how in spite of your bereavement and loneliness you reach out your hands in ministry to those who need aid, comfort and renewal of life. It is indeed a privilege for me to know Dr. Anderson and to have him write about the wonderful breakthroughs which he and his associates are making in the war against preventable loss of sight. With affectionate greetings, I am. Sincerely your friend.[13]

Mab's motivations in aiding the visually impaired are unknown, but Keller's letter suggests that this cause remained close to Mab's heart even after Russell's death. Mab's sense of duty to help those 'less fortunate'—a powerful shared value for the couple—may have been heightened by her husband's passing.

THE FITZROY MISSION FREE KINDERGARTEN

Perhaps Mab's greatest achievement in the world of volunteer organising was serving as president of the Fitzroy Mission Free Kindergarten (renamed the Isabel Henderson Kindergarten in 1949) from about 1946 to at least 1955. She remained part of the central organising body for the Free Kindergarten Movement, the Free Kindergarten Union of Victoria (FKUV), well into the 1960s.

The Fitzroy Mission Free Kindergarten was one of around thirty pre-schools affiliated with the FKUV. When Mab became associated with the union during the 1940s, the organisation had been operating for decades. Established in 1908 by a group of middle-class educated women to unite all free kindergartens in Victoria and provide standardised training for kindergarten teachers, the FKUV incorporated both educational and philanthropic aims. It was born out of Melbourne's early Kindergarten Movement and philanthropic and religious welfare initiatives. The Kindergarten Movement, which emerged during the mid-nineteenth century in Europe, was based on principles of the German educator Fredrich Frobel (1782–1852). His 'Kindergarten Method' was founded on the belief that preschool-aged children required training from an early age and that their educators should be properly trained to foster gradual growth in kindergarteners. He believed that children should be provided with an adequate climate in which to flourish and grow, an environment that included 'suitable places for rest, suitable equipment … gentle direction', which would foster their early development and prepare them for schooling.[14] Frobel's teachings provided a theoretical framework for the Kindergarten Movement that developed throughout the late nineteenth century and into the twentieth century in Australia.

'New Education' policies flourished across early-twentieth-century Australia and resulted in an expanding recognition of the need for preschool education and teacher training. Educational leaders in Victoria envisaged a group of kindergartens that could be used as practical training centres for prospective teachers and could provide free early childhood education for underprivileged children.

'International House Given Large Cheque', *The Argus*, 1 July 1953.

The FKUV's first meeting took place in October 1908 under the supervision of Emmeline Pye, head of Central Brunswick State School; the principal of the Melbourne Teachers' College, John Smyth; and Annie Westmoreland, who had opened one of the earliest kindergarten training schools, in Kew. From its beginnings, the union incorporated social welfare initiatives in its aims, providing support and financial assistance to its affiliated kindergartens. Indeed, many of its founders were motivated by a concern for children who lived in the densely populated streets and insanitary dwellings of Melbourne's inner city and suburbs. There was some tension between the educationalist and philanthropic wings of the organisation, with the former emphasising teacher training and education, the latter 'child rescue' and charity work. Mab's motivations for joining the FKUV were most likely philanthropic in nature, yet she advocated for teacher training as essential to the development and 'protection' of children. Her activities as president of the Fitzroy Mission Free Kindergarten emphasised volunteerism and charity work as cornerstones.

The Fitzroy Mission Free Kindergarten was established in 1913 by wealthy women from Melbourne's south-eastern suburbs in conjunction with Presbyterian missionaries in Fitzroy. The kindergarten committee oversaw the provision of essential items for local families, in addition to conducting home visits and giving lectures on diet, health and hygiene. Throughout the first half of the twentieth century, despite suffering intermittent financial distress, the organisation provided education and support to the local community.

In the aftermath of the Great Depression and World War II, the Fitzroy Mission Free Kindergarten was in economic turmoil. Mab became president of the committee in the 1940s during a period of financial difficulty for the FKUV more generally. The local committees responsible for affiliated kindergartens were struggling to remain self-sufficient and were relying on FKUV funding to stay afloat. At the same time, non-affiliated kindergartens were developing across Melbourne, mostly in association with churches, creating competition for FKUV affiliates.

In a letter to *The Herald* in 1946, Mab expressed her concern for the lack of funding her committee had received that year. In the letter, she refers to an article published in *The Herald* called 'Children of the Poor', written by Rohan Rivett, an acclaimed Australian author and journalist, on the 'vicious and disgraceful' living conditions of impoverished families in Melbourne's inner suburbs. Rivett described the streets and dwellings of Fitzroy, a working-class neighbourhood, as cramped and unliveable, with Melbourne's 'slum children' the greatest victims.[15] Responding to the article, Mab wrote:

> The Fitzroy Mission Free Kindergarten, among others, is doing what it can with inadequate funds to alleviate this situation. For many years efforts have been made to secure a site of our own on which to erect a modern kindergarten building for the extension of our work. These efforts have proved unsuccessful and we have recently been told that even were a site available we would not be allowed to build at present. So we are compelled to carry on in premises unsuitable and too small, which are generously lent to us free of charge by the Mission.[16]

Over the next three years, Mab and the Fitzroy Mission Free Kindergarten committee devoted their time to fundraising and lobbying the mayor and local councillors of Fitzroy for the building of a new kindergarten in the area. At the thirty-fourth annual meeting of the Fitzroy Mission Free Kindergarten in October 1947, Mab announced that '£3,260 had been raised for the Kindergarten Building Fund by a raffle of a Hillman Minx Sedan'.[17] The committee had also negotiated with local government to make a section of land available for the new building. In 1949, the foundations were laid for the Isabel Henderson Kindergarten at the Green Reserve in Fitzroy, designed to accommodate sixty children. The ceremony was reported in the press with an image of Mab and the all-female committee, along with the mayoress of Fitzroy, Mrs R Solomon.[18]

The FKUV was a female-dominated philanthropic organisation made up of women of all classes and professional backgrounds, yet the leadership roles were mostly exercised by wealthy patrons. Indeed, the FKUV was one of the primary philanthropic causes that elite women in Melbourne were drawn to during the first half of the twentieth century. As Swain points out, while upper-class women gained status from associating their name with philanthropic and educational organisations such as the FKUV, it was often middle-class women who provided the labour that kept such organisations afloat.[19] However, women such as Mab provided an essential financial and organisational contribution to the movement by establishing the FKUV's status and relevance among Melbourne's upper class. Indeed, Mab held innumerable fundraising events for the Fitzroy Mission Free Kindergarten that helped to circulate information about the movement and raise money for the kindergarten.

In the world of wealthy women's philanthropy, charity and organisational work during the early twentieth century, we can see the creation of a sphere that bridged the public and the private, belonging to women and their expertise. In the case of the Free Kindergarten Movement, this was a cause that centred upon the welfare of poor women and children, resulting in concrete changes and support for families in need. Mab continued to provide financial assistance to the Isabel Henderson Kindergarten until she died.

THE RUSSELL GRIMWADE SCHOOL OF BIOCHEMISTRY

On 16 April 1958, Mab declared open the first stage of the Russell Grimwade Building for the School of Biochemistry and Molecular Biology at the University of Melbourne.[20] She played an indispensable role in opening the first stage of the school, situated in the university's new medical precinct opposite Royal Melbourne Hospital. The building had been a project of Russell's prior to his death, and he had provided £50,000 for it in 1944. Eager to fulfil her husband's wishes, Mab gave £20,000 to the project in 1957. Frustrated with the lack of progress made on the building, she provided a further £20,000 in 1958 on the condition that work would commence on its second part in 1959. Speaking to a crowd that included the university's vice-chancellor, the Victorian premier and the Nobel Prize–winning neurophysiologist John Eccles, she expressed that she was 'so happy and proud to be here today and also sad that my husband couldn't be here to see his Biochemistry School'. The school would be a 'fitting memorial to him … especially when it is finished'. Mab conveyed her hopes for the school in the future, invoking the words of the Queen Mother on her recent visit to the university in March 1958:

> I think the Queen Mother said in her address here that Melbourne had been fortunate in her University and that she hoped its achievements in its second century would exceed those of the first. So I hope this School may help and do its part.

Principals in the ceremony of turning the first sod of the foundations of the Isabel Henderson Free Kindergarten at the Green Reserve, Fitzroy, yesterday were (from left): The mayoress of Fitzroy (Mrs. R. Solomons), Mr. H. O'Halloran, Mrs. Russell Grimwade, Mrs. Chester Guest and Mrs. B. Sawyer.

'Principles in the Ceremony', *The Age*, 4 June 1949.

The opening of the Biochemistry Building marked the culmination of a lifetime of philanthropy and charity work for Mab. It was a testament to her husband's interests and philanthropic work, and to her commitment to improving the future of Victorian society. To ensure Russell's dream was kept alive, she dedicated another £40,000 to the building in her will.

•

After Russell's death, Mab continued to provide financial assistance and gifts to charitable, artistic and educational institutions. The receipts, letters and notebooks from her papers indicate the generous donations she made to various institutions from 1957 to 1965, including Boys' and Girls' clubs, the University of Melbourne, the Braille Library of Victoria, the International House Building Fund, the Commonwealth Scientific and Industrial Research Organisation, the Australian National Memorial, the Theatre Building Fund and the Victorian Society for the Prevention of Cruelty to Children.

In 1959 she donated £50,000 to the state government's Cultural Centre building appeal, consolidating her commitment to Victoria's artistic community; in acknowledgement, the National Gallery of Victoria's gardens were named the Russell Grimwade Gardens. In 1962, she was made a Commander of the Order of the British Empire for her service to charities. The Miegunyah Fund and Bequests would be her final philanthropic contribution, confirming her as a pillar of the Australian philanthropic community. For Mab, as for her peers, philanthropy and charity work provided opportunities for the exercise of influence and social power, organisational talent and a sense of altruism, while helping to shape the society of Victoria.

Chapter 5.

THE MAB GRIMWADE CUP

'Montalto Cricket Team', *Table Talk*, 20 April 1905.

'An early start at the 10th hole at the Hotel Links ... Such pretty links with beautiful fairways with dozens of sprinklers going everywhere. Slightly easier than Cable Beach. Our play was very bad.'

MAB GRIMWADE 1923

In 1905, Mabel Kelly was the captain of Toorak's Montalto cricket team. That year, they played two heated games against the Geelong Ladies' Cricket Club. *The Age* reported that Montalto lost the first game, played in Melbourne, but in the second, played a fortnight later in the grounds of Geelong College, the Toorak team 'had its revenge', winning 212 to 67.[1] A photograph of the Montalto team was published in *Table Talk* the following month, showing Mab firmly holding a cricket bat, two seats away from her cousin Gladys.[2] The girls are wearing restrictive uniforms characteristic of contemporary women's sporting garments, including a heavy white cotton serge ankle-length skirt, a billowing blouse fastened with a belt, a tie, and a cumbersome cabbage-tree hat. From the late nineteenth century, rational dress reform had loosened the social codes on sporting attire for women, yet female cricket players were expected to maintain a 'feminine' image to counteract the masculine associations of the game.

While Montalto was establishing itself as a successful girls' cricket team, Mab was elected as president of the Yarraville Cricket Club, a male-dominated junior club. She was elected as the only female member of the club for her outstanding ability, having played 'first class cricket' the previous year.[3] That an eighteen-year-old Mabel Kelly was elected president of a co-ed cricket club speaks to both her athletic talent and her capacity for leadership from a young age. Moreover, her participation in competitive cricket was relatively unusual for a woman, even during the early twentieth century. While hockey, lawn tennis and croquet were deemed acceptable and legitimate 'feminine' sports, cricket was traditionally associated with typically 'masculine' physical traits, such as strength and agility.

Mab maintained an interest in sport throughout her life and proved herself an accomplished sportswoman. Apart from cricket, she enjoyed a range of sports inherited from the British social elite, including golf, tennis and punting. She was also a patron of many sporting events, attending and organising race meets and polo competitions. She loved horses and presented her brother Charles with several outstanding polo ponies.

Mab grew up in a familial and institutional environment where sport, physical activity and competition were encouraged. She played cricket with her brothers who were, like her, keen cricketers, and benefited from the introduction of physical education into school curriculums from the 1870s. Physical education was encouraged at private secondary girls' schools when anxieties that sport was detrimental to women's reproductive capacities were superseded by a belief that physical activity was essential to female development. For girls attending one of the largest private secondary girls' schools in Victoria, Presbyterian Ladies' College, sports were 'encouraged and practised, and every girl pressed to take part in them'.[4] The facilities of such schools allowed for students to be taught a variety of physical exercises, including gymnastics, drill exercises, swimming, rowing and physical culture, and they could play organised team sports such as tennis, croquet, hockey, baseball, lacrosse and cricket. Oberwyl, the private girls' school Mab most likely attended, offered gymnastic classes from at least 1886; by the early twentieth century, its students were part of a statewide 'Ladies' School Singles Championship' for lawn tennis.[5]

The shift in attitudes regarding women's physical activity contributed to the evolution of amateur women's sport teams in Australia. As a journalist wrote in the *Adelaide Observer* in 1885, 'in one branch of life, that of sport, the woman of the present day not only theoretically but also practically has established her right to take a share as well as an interest'.[6] By the early twentieth century, competitive sport had become a popular activity among women and for a young Mabel Kelly. Sports clubs and associations were formed to represent the growing number of women interested in team sport. The Victorian Ladies' Cricket Association (VLCA) was established in 1905 as the first women's cricket association in Australia. Initially, it represented twenty-one Victorian teams and was presided over by the famous Victorian suffragist Vida Goldstein. In Melbourne, cricket retained its middle- and upper-class associations, and women's cricket teams were mostly clustered in the wealthy south and south-eastern suburbs. By 1907 there were as many as forty teams, composed of around 400 female players.[7] However, women were not encouraged to professionalise as sportspeople in general: sport was viewed as a form of recreation for unmarried middle- and upper-class girls and women, and some sports were encouraged more than others.

While World War I instigated a temporary decline in organised women's sport, by the 1920s, as women's participation in the public sphere grew, so did opportunities for them in sport. In the wake of the Great War, new imperatives for women's health and fitness arose amid fears of 'racial degeneration' and a declining birthrate. Competitive sports were formalised at local and national levels, and networks were established among female administrators in each state. In 1931, the Australian Women's Cricket Council became the formal organising body for all state-level women's cricketing associations in the country.

While female sporting associations were termed 'ladies' associations' prior to World War I, women's expanding role in postwar society meant that the term 'women' became used more commonly for female sporting clubs. In the media, the modern sportswoman was represented as 'educated, independent, fashionable, thin and athletic' and sport was viewed as an acceptable activity for middle-class women.[8] Mab's interest in cricket appears to have waned upon her marriage to Russell, and halted altogether during wartime, perhaps due to the persistent associations between masculinity and cricket. After the war, she continued to foster her competitive nature and her interest in sport through a lifelong dedication to the game of golf.

GOLF

Mab pursued golf as a recreational activity and occasionally as a competitive sport. In 1917 she joined Melbourne's most prestigious golfing institution, the Royal Melbourne Golf Club (RMGC). In the following years she quickly formalised her position there, establishing herself on the council of the associates in 1924 (at that time women were called 'associates' and men were 'members'), becoming vice president from 1930 to 1932 and then president from 1933 to 1935. During her time as vice president, she instituted an annual trophy for the associates for a foursome's matchplay on handicap; she called it the

Mab Grimwade Cup. She shared her love of golf with Russell, and they played together at courses not only in Melbourne and at the so-called Millionaires Golf Club near their property in Frankston, but also at some of the finest golf courses across Australia and the globe. Mab teed off at Auckland Golf Club Middlemore in New Zealand's North Island, enjoyed links across India, Ceylon and British Columbia, surveyed Hawaii's famous cliffside links, and toured courses across California and the west coast of the United States. Her travel diaries during the 1920s are filled with detailed portrayals of every rolling green she played on or simply saw from the comfort of a luxury motor car.

In the interwar period, as international golf networks and competitions expanded, it was increasingly common for elite golfing enthusiasts of Victoria to tour and compete on courses around the world. Female golfers were at the forefront of this phenomenon, playing both recreationally and in championships mostly in Britain and the United States. During her travels, Mab played only recreationally, preferring to observe the lush surroundings and enjoy each round at a leisurely pace with caddies in tow. On a trip to Honolulu in July 1923 at the beginning of the Grimwades' 'American Adventure', she commended the scenic golf courses there, which she enjoyed both with Russell and alone. On 21 July, after taking a 'beautiful drive' to the Nuʻuanu Pali cliffside lookout along the Honolulu coast, the couple 'had tea at the Country Club a charming spot and fascinating Club House & golf links in the most wonderful setting amongst the Hills'.[9] Later in the month while in Ontario, Canada, Mab 'set out independently after breakfast for the Oak Bay Golf Links 4 miles [6.4 kilometres] out'. She enjoyed the 'charming tricky links' and the impressive scenery overlooking the 'Olympic snow-capped mts in the distance'.

The Grimwades' transpacific adventure was clearly taken relatively early in Mab's golfing career, and she emphasised her inexperience with foreign courses and difficult terrain. In America, she and Russell toured the links at every place they stayed, from the San Francisco Golf Club to the 'delightful' La Cumbre Golf and Country Club in Santa Barbara, and then up the west coast to the 'ripping' courses at Portland's Colwood Golf Links. Arriving in San Francisco in August, Mab described insufficient links at the golf club, lamenting the lack of 'ladies' tees', which were traditionally shortened, and expressing

Opposite, Mab playing golf at Miegunyah, 1918.
Following spread, Mab playing golf at Westerfield, November 1929.

her lack of confidence playing on American golf links: 'Left at 8.40 to the San Francisco Golf Club for a game feeling very shy about it—secured two new caddies ... Quite difficult ... & narrow fairways. No ladies tees ...'

Later that month as the pair made their way around the San Francisco Peninsula, Mab continued to express trepidation about American competitions, commenting that she and Russell were 'too shy' to enter the 'Midsummer Golf Tournament' at their hotel and instead played poorly at the hotel links:

> An early start at the 10th hole at the Hotel Links to avoid the match tournament. Such pretty links with beautiful fairways with dozens of sprinklers going everywhere. Slightly easier than Cable Beach. Our play was very bad. After lunch went to a Polo match in which Drury, Hitchcock & A Driscoll were playing. A very fast game & beautiful ponies. Tea at the Links & another 9 holes.

Mab's entries reveal the pleasure and excitement she found not only in playing golf but in the ritual surrounding the game: finding the best links in the area, assessing the environment and the landscape, playing several rounds, and finally taking tea in the clubrooms and socialising with friends and locals. This was a sport suited to the social elite, one that did not demand extreme physical exertion and could be played only by those with disposable income and extensive leisure time.

•

In Australia, golf, like cricket, was a successful British import. Victoria boasted the country's best golfing terrain, with its undulating hills and sandy soil and vegetation reminiscent of the Scottish coastal fairways where the modern game was developed. The sport was pioneered by Scottish migrants in the Antipodes, and the first instance of organised golf in Victoria took place during the 1840s; full-time club golf emerged during the last decade of the nineteenth century. By this time, its requisite expensive materials and extended leisure time meant the sport became the preserve of the wealthy. Indeed, golfing, described by the *Geelong Advertiser* as 'the most fashionable game in Great Britain', became largely popular among Victoria's elite as a recreational exercise, and later for competition.[10]

The Melbourne Golf Club, which became the Royal Melbourne Golf Club, was established in 1891 as one of the first formal golf clubs in Australia.

Its opening at the links on the Emo Estate in Caulfield defined the club and the sport itself as a game for the genteel classes and, for the most part, for 'gentlemen'. *The Australasian* made the game's social make-up very clear: 'At the close of the play the competitors in twos make for the club-house ... the bankers, merchants, and barristers resume the habits and speech of civilized life to discuss the incidents of the day, and apply the law to doubtful cases'.[11] The clubrooms were housed in a newly built villa and included a large dining room, a smoking room, a spacious kitchen and a 'golf parlour'.[12] While the opening of the club included around 100 'gentlemen', women were admitted entry as players immediately, becoming a crucial part of Victorian golfing culture from the late nineteenth century.

In August 1894 the first Australian Ladies' Amateur Championship was held in Victoria by the Melbourne and Geelong clubs, making it one of the oldest golf championships for women in the world. By 1895 women were enrolled in golf clubs across Australia, and in 1898 the Australian Golf Union was controlling both women's and men's golf. While golf was deemed an acceptable sport for women as it did not challenge 'appropriate' feminine behaviour, club constitutions and regulations dictated several restrictions on their participation in the game. From its beginnings in the early nineteenth century, women were called 'associates' and men were 'members'. In the early twentieth century at the RMGC, women were excluded from access to the golf course on the afternoons of Wednesdays, Saturdays and public holidays. Dan Soutar, the pioneer of professional golf in Australia, wrote on women golfers in 1905, illustrating the prevailing attitudes: 'women with a handicap of not more than five strokes should, I think, be allowed to play over the men's courses at will, except on Saturdays and public holidays, it being understood that they should always be willing to allow men, coming on behind, to pass them, if the latter so desired'.[13] The ideology underpinning the regulation of women's practice hinged on the belief that women were less talented than male players and should always defer to their male counterparts on the golf course. According to historian Jane Senyard, while the sport was viewed as a 'natural arena of male accomplishment', women's golf was often associated with amateurism and a lack of rational understanding of the game.[14]

Following spread, Del Monte Links in California, August 1924.

Golf clubs were also gender segregated, allotting separate clubs for female members, not allowing women to play alongside men, and giving women shortened golf tees. From the 1890s, the women's club at the RMGC was presided over by the wives of prominent elite men, including Mrs JM (Mary) Bruce, the mother of Stanley Bruce, the future prime minister of Australia. From this time, women staged their own competitions at local, state and interstate levels. In 1906, women golfers formed their own statewide union, the Victorian Ladies' Golf Union. It was not until 1921 that national and international women's competitions were controlled by the Australian Ladies Golf Union, championed by its president, Lady Halse Rodgers.[15] From the 1920s, Mab took an active role in Victoria's culture of golf. In her administrative roles as council member, vice president and president of the associates at the RMGC, she helped to support women's competitive golf through the Mab Grimwade Cup. As she became embedded in the Victorian golfing community, women's golf—and the sport more generally—entered a 'golden era'.

THE MAB GRIMWADE CUP

As Victoria emerged from the Depression in the 1930s, women's sport was experiencing a 'boom'.[16] Throughout the postwar period golf had undergone a transformation, with improved courses attracting a greater number of women than men to the sport. A new urgency to expand women's golfing practice resulted in the first course in Victoria based on equality between men and women, in Glen Waverley, being formed. The 1920s ushered in a 'new breed' of female competitive golfers in Victoria, with players such as Gladys Hay, Mona MacLeod and Susie Tolhurst dominating the Victorian women's championships.[17] The success of female players meant that women were more widely accepted as professional and competitive; the first interstate women's match was played in 1933 and won by Victoria.

The Mab Grimwade Cup flourished in its first decade as the popularity of women's competitions grew. The championship extended over the season, with fixed dates for the rounds, and culminated in a celebratory tea party for contestants. The trophy itself is an imposing silver wine cooler made of silverplate and copper, dated to c. 1869. In 1957, Mab gave a £60 endowment for the trophy, consolidating her commitment to its longevity. Today it is the largest trophy in the women's cabinets at the RMGC.[18]

The first competition for the Mab Grimwade Cup was played in October 1930, and the names of the winners were published in *The Argus*.[19] The following year, the trophy attracted some of the best female players in the country:

> The replicas of the Mab Grimwade Cup, at Royal Melbourne, are destined to go into the possession of either the Misses Susie and Shirley Tolhurst or Mrs Fred Fairbairn and Miss C. Lascelles, who up to date have accounted for all comers. It must be finalised before next Friday, when the final medal and competition day of the season is listed.[20]

During the interwar period, the RMGC was home to the most talented concentration of female golfers in Australia. The finalists for the Mab Grimwade Cup, all associate members at the RMGC, were widely known for their extraordinary hitting power and low handicaps. By the mid 1930s, Susie Tolhurst had won two Australian championships and five Victorian titles and was being lauded by the press as 'Australia's best woman golfer'.[21] Her sister Shirley Tolhurst had won the junior Victorian title in 1926 at the age of eighteen and beat Susie for the state title in 1934; by 1937, she had the lowest handicap in Victoria among women golfers.[22] Cicely Lascelles, although not as widely known as the Tolhurst sisters, had been on the women's competitive golfing scene from 1915, when she entered her first major tournament in Geelong. While Lascelles never chose to turn professional, she was a highly influential figure, representing both Victoria and Australia on a number of occasions within the country and internationally. In 1922, she instituted the Lascelles Cup for associate members at the RMGC, an annual event played with one stroke round (a form of competition where players attempt to secure the fewest total number of strokes by the end of the round), leading to the first sixteen lowest scorers qualifying for matchplay against competitors on a hole-to-hole basis.[23]

Like Lascelles and the Tolhursts, Mab was not only a patron of golf but also a regular player. She occasionally entered amateur competitions and in 1933 was pictured in *The Herald* looking cheery as she waited for the first tee in the women's foursome handicap alongside 'Miss P. Leary, Miss D. Cawlishaw, Mrs I. B. Cox, and Mrs Lionel Hood'.[24]

While Mab never pursued golf as a full-time profession, she used the sport to foster her social relationships and fundraising networks. As president of the associates at RMGC, she organised numerous 'golf gymkhanas' and tea parties to support charitable causes and facilitate socialising between married and unmarried female golfers. The tea parties were typically feminine social occasions used to mark events on the golfing calendar. In 1934, the opening day of the season for the associates was celebrated with an extravagant afternoon tea in the women's lounge organised by Mab, who ensured the clubrooms were filled with vibrant flower arrangements.[25] The network of associates and council members Mab cultivated also provided her with an avenue for socialising and fundraising. In August 1933, a meeting held at Miegunyah for the upcoming 'golf gymkhana' organised by Mab was reported on in *The Argus*:

> Mrs. Russell Grimwade, president of the associates of the Royal Melbourne Golf Club, convened a meeting on Tuesday afternoon at her home, Orrong Rd Toorak, to discuss plans for the gymkhana to be held by the associates on October 31 in aid of the special appeal for £10,000 for the Melbourne District Nursing Society. The meeting was held in the entrance hall, where creamy lilies were grouped with charming effect against the dark paneled wall, and afterwards Mrs. Grimwade entertained all those present at tea. The Misses Nancy Walsh and Marcia Ross were appointed joint honorary secretary and treasurer.

In her role as player, administrator and leader, Mab helped to expand the place of women in the elite culture of Victorian golf. Within this culture, however, distinctions between 'ladies' and 'gentlemen' players persisted through the twentieth century. It was not until 1984 that women were entitled to play on Wednesday and Saturday afternoons on all Victorian golf courses, due to the passage of equal opportunity legislation. By that time golf had become more accessible to all, and Victoria's courses were being enjoyed by men and women from all walks of life.

•

For Mab, sport was a source of pleasure and recreation, an outlet for her competitive energies, the basis of a vital social network, an avenue for philanthropy and charity work, and, importantly, a realm in which she excelled as

'Women's Foursomes at Royal Melbourne', *The Herald*, 15 May 1933.

an administrator and a leader from a young age. From being president of the Yarraville Cricket Club at age eighteen to president of the associates at RMGC as an older married woman, her administrative and leadership roles reveal another part of her life in which she developed her interests into formal positions where she could organise, manage and lead.

Mab's involvement in sport also fits within larger narratives of Australian women in sport, and of the fight for women to be included in social and professional activities hitherto deemed suitable only for men. As sport historian Greg Ryan puts it, 'women's sport succeeded because women wanted it, and, equally importantly, were prepared to administer and fund it'.[26] While it is unlikely Mab pursued sport as an act of feminist defiance, she did play a small but significant part in the advancement of women in sport through her participation in cricket teams, a sport not commonly associated with femininity, to becoming an administrator and a patron of women's golf. The Mab Grimwade Cup remains a prestigious annual tournament to this day, and the names of the winners since 1930 are listed on a board in the Women's Sitting Room at the RMGC. The cup is a fitting emblem of Mab's contribution to the Victorian golfing community.

Chapter 6.

THE MAB GRIMWADE ROSE

'To Mab, for whom the Flowers grow.'

RUSSELL GRIMWADE, DEDICATION IN HIS
BOOK *ANTHOLOGY OF THE EUCALYPTS*, 1920

In 1937, Russell Grimwade registered a sport[1] of rosarian Alister Clark's 'Lorraine Lee' rose, named 'Mrs Russell Grimwade', with the National Rose Society of Victoria.[2] The 'Mrs. Russell Grimwade'—or 'Mab Grimwade' rose, as it was widely known—was most likely developed in Westerfield's rose garden.[3] Its petals boast a richer fuchsia-pink than the original 'Lorraine Lee', Clark's most famous and widely planted rose. That year, Clark (1864-1949) described the variety in the horticulture publication *The Australian Rose Annual*: 'This beautiful bush Rose carries quantities of rich orange flowers of a shade rather difficult to describe. It is very free and constantly in bloom and is sent out after thorough testing for Australian conditions.'[4]

In the same year, Clark presented his new list of roses to the National Rose Society of Victoria, to be displayed at the society's annual show at Melbourne Town Hall. Each variety was given the name of a prominent Victorian woman. *The Herald* reported on the occasion:

> As usual, Mr. Clark has paid a compliment to Melbourne women in naming his new blooms, and those of us who go down to the show tomorrow will be pleased to see entirely new roses under such familiar names as Mab Grimwade, Ella Guthrie, Sheila Bellair, Fairlie Rede, Doris Osbourne, Sophie Mackinnion ... Gwendoline Collins [and] Lady Huntingford.[5]

Opposite, Mab gardening at Westerfield, October 1929.

After their display at the town hall, the roses were distributed to nurserymen, seedsmen and florists across Victoria in hopes that they would 'enrich gardening wherever they are grown'.[6] The 'Mab Grimwade' seedling was swiftly bought and distributed by one of the leading seed merchants in Victoria, Law, Somner Pty Ltd.[7] In 1938, the rose was displayed for a second time at the National Rose Society's autumn show, and was noted in the press as 'one of the most interesting [roses] exhibited':

> The new rose has all the characteristics and habits of growth of its famous parent [the Lorraine Lee] and has the valuable attraction of flowering all the year round. It is at its best when other roses are not in flower, particularly in the winter months of the year. It is a deep fuchsia pink in color. Rosarians expect this variety to prove an acquisition to the list of Australia-raised roses.[8]

The 1938 *Australian Rose Annual* noted that the 'Mab Grimwade' had made its way to New Zealand and was listed as a favourite of the New Zealand Rose Society.[9] The following year it was among the 'modern varieties' displayed at the National Rose Show in Victoria, an event attended by over 3000 people.[10]

The reach of Alister Clark's roses extended across a network of rose societies in the United States, New Zealand and Britain. Clark, acknowledged as Australia's 'Man of Roses', was the most renowned rosarian in the country during the early twentieth century. He was a foundational member of the National Rose Society of Victoria, and in 1936 was awarded the Dean Hole Medal by the National Rose Society in London for his services to the culture of roses. His pastoral property at Glenara, Bulla, immortalised in an 1867 painting by Eugene von Guerard hung at the National Gallery of Victoria, provided the home soil for his rose seedlings. An article in *The Australasian* reported on Glenara's offerings in the 1938 *Australian Rose Annual*, including Mab's namesake:

> Mr. Alister Clark takes the reader for a walk around his garden at Glenara, Bulla (V.), a garden from which some of the loveliest roses grown to-day have emanated. There the first blooms of Black Boy, Sunny South, Lorraine Lee, Lady Stradbroke, and many another lovely seedling raised by Mr. Clark opened its petals to be appraised, tried out, retained, or discarded. Writing of some of the varieties growing to-day in his garden, he says: 'Zuru Hore Ruthven makes

Eric Timewell, The 'Mab Grimwade' rose, February 2014.

bushes of 6ft. [1.8 metres], and its long stems are crowned with really beautiful flowers, well held, and of a fine rich pink. Mab Grimwade also likes this old bed, in spite of tree roots.'[11]

The rose seedlings Clark produced at Glenara became immensely popular during the 1920s and 1930s, commended in the press for their brilliant colour and vigour. Clark applied a conservationist approach to gardening, and crossbred roses that suited the dry and hot Australian climate.[12] His seedlings were hybrid creations, bred from *Rosa gigantea*, an indigenous Chinese climbing shrub with large single white flowers, grown in Burma and the Himalayas and suited to humid climates. East Asian roses such as *Rosa gigantea* embodied what rose breeders viewed as the four most important plant characteristics: 'vigour, fragrance, colour variation, and a long period of flowering'.[13] Such breeds helped to transform old European garden roses into the classic hybrid teas that we know today. Clark was at the forefront of rose breeding, ensuring his seedlings grew in favourable ambient conditions and abstaining from using chemical pesticides, preferring the use of birds to prevent disease—the birds would eat plant-eroding aphids off his roses. Once a seedling had been carefully tested, he would present a new rose to one of the national rose societies and receive the profit from its first year of sales.

Clark's roses were at their height of popularity during the decades between the world wars, reflecting the general vogue for roses in Western Europe and the United States during this period. In the early twentieth century, the rose became a powerful symbol for national characteristics, working-class rebellions and the union of romance and violence.[14] It was a common feature of poems, artworks and designs as well as an elegant accessory for gentlemen and ladies. The wild rose evoked the romance of rebellion and liberty for the English poet Rupert Brooke, while the domesticated rose garden provided an idealistic symbol for working-class women activists in the United States.[15] During this time, rose-naming became increasingly commercialised as new laws came to dictate the patenting of rose names. Yet naming practices continued to follow the nineteenth-century tradition of naming roses after upper-class women, a gesture of honour for a woman or her influential husband. In the twentieth century, strategic naming practices increased the chance of a seedling's commercial success. The right name could conjure up an image of glamour and sophistication, capitalising on the cultural association between femininity, beauty and flowers. Other seedling names embodied Clark's nationalist impulses, including 'Australia Felix' (1919), 'Squatter's Dream' (1927), 'Billy Boiler' (1927) and 'Southern Cross' (1931).

Sixty-five women gave their names to Clark's roses, among them some of the most significant members of Australia's and New Zealand's patriciate. Entries included Margaret Eleanor Crosby or 'Lady Huntingfield', the wife of Victoria's governor; Zara Hore Ruthven, or 'Lady Gowrie', the wife of Australia's governor-general; and other women titled either by birth or by marriage, along with community activists, artists and amateur sportswomen.[16] Despite their diversity of interests, the women shared several defining characteristics: they came from significant local or British families, they were privately educated in the Antipodes or Europe, and they had either married an influential politically or commercially successful figure or remained single, dedicating their lives to philanthropy and charity work. That Mab Grimwade's name appeared among these influential women speaks to her standing within Melbourne's social elite, and the prestige her name could contribute to a rose's commercial value.

Clark's roses, and rose breeding more generally, lost popularity during World War II due to the lack of resources to fund commercial nurseries. Today, Clark's roses can be found in a number of public and private gardens across Victoria, and the Alister Clark Memorial Rose Garden in Bulla commemorates his influence on Australian horticulture. Mab herself was associated with the establishment of a memorial rose garden to Clark after his death that would be 'worthy of Melbourne and worthy of the memory of the man whose memory it would perpetuate'.[17] While his seedlings are now slowly being revived, in the interwar period they could be found across Australia in the gardens of great estates and suburban backyards alike.

Roses were an essential part of Australian gardens from the nineteenth century, reflecting the important role European gardening practices played in shaping the settler landscape and progressing the settler–colonial project. From the early years of colonisation, gardening provided a vital source of recreation and a powerful tool of place making for settlers. Over time, it became a cultural expression of the national imaginary, and by the twentieth century the suburban house and garden had become an emblem of the 'Australian dream'.[18] Horticultural writing during this period advocated for the garden as a crucial site for forging citizenship, a space in which the 'citizen gardener' could be made and remade. A mown lawn, a manicured hedge and a pruned rose garden were signs of good citizenship, national belonging and loyalty to Empire. Gardens were, and still are, powerful cultural symbols, containing expressions of class and gender identities that reflect prevailing social attitudes. Men were traditionally associated with the phenomenon of the 'citizen gardener'; however, many women were the architects of their own gardens. Often, married couples worked together to cultivate their ideal home environment.[19]

MIEGUNYAH'S GARDEN

Mab and Russell were among the millions of Australians whose gardens were at once a source of personal pleasure and a setting for the cultivation of a sense of place and belonging. The couple implemented their ideal garden landscapes at Miegunyah and Westerfield. Their gardens were sites of production, consumption and recreation, and an expression of Mab and Russell's imaginations and horticultural interests.

The expansive formal gardens at Miegunyah grew substantially over time through a series of extensions and alterations, developing, as John Poynter notes, 'from the notable to the superb'.[20] Miegunyah's garden combined beauty with functionality and a reverence for both European and Australian garden design. Katja Wager describes it at its finest: 'It incorporated a series of Australian Arts and Crafts sunken "rooms", a pond, English vernacular masonry and Italianate elements ... in addition to a productive kitchen garden, rose beds and a carefully maintained eucalypt arboretum.'[21]

The design reflected early-twentieth-century European and Australian trends and the Grimwades' passion for environmental sustainability and the conservation of native plants. The decorative garden was a pursuit of the moneyed elite from the mid nineteenth century; it was a product of leisure and the labour of full-time gardeners, signifying wealth, status and national pride. In Melbourne, the social elite worked with landscape architects and garden designers to ensure the beauty and sustainability of their expansive private

Opposite, View of the garden at Miegunyah, September 1917.

gardens. While Russell himself is credited with much of Miegunyah's garden design, the architects and designers who contributed to its construction and alterations were some of the most successful of their day, including Edna Walling, Ellis Stones, EF Cook, John Stevens and WH Griffiths.[22]

Walling, one of the most celebrated garden designers in Australia, helped to encourage women's representation in professional horticulture during the early twentieth century. She was unique in that she encouraged the use of native plants in her garden designs in the later part of her career. However, her early style was heavily influenced by the structure and formality of the Italian Renaissance, and it is perhaps to her that we owe some of Miegunyah's Italianate elements. It has also been suggested that she was partly responsible for the informal English garden that stretched across the Selbourne Road boundary of the property. Walling's designs resonated with many of Toorak's wealthy residents, and she helped to design many gardens in that area along with Victorian country properties and sections of the Melbourne Zoological Gardens.[23]

Stones, whose work was supported by Walling, worked collaboratively with Russell on many of Miegunyah's garden elements. He was a conservationist and an early proponent of the use of Australian native plants in garden design, his style shaping the future of Australian landscaping. Stones' lasting influence can be found in several of Miegunyah's sunken gardens and in its stone-paved pond with the bronze sculpture named for the Grimwades' niece Amanda at its centre. In an essay to his young niece, Russell narrated the construction of the pond: 'Aunt and Uncle have a garden. It is a nice garden with things in it, like trees and grass and hoses and both dogs running about in it. Billibully is the gardener, and he is very fond of digging … And that's how the pond came to be made.'[24]

Its significant size, unique design and diversity of European and native plants made the Miegunyah garden one of the finest private gardens in Victoria. In the 1950s, images of it and other private gardens were featured in the pages of the *Australian Women's Weekly*, providing amateur gardeners with 'planting ideas for every type of garden, large or small'.[25] By studying the advice and the detailed images provided by the *Women's Weekly* and other women's and

Opposite, *Statue of Amanda*, unknown.
Following spread, Mab gardening at Westerfield, December 1925.

gardening magazines, elements of Victoria's first-class gardens could be replicated in backyards across the country.

From the 1920s, Westerfield's sprawling property became the rural counterpart to Miegunyah's urban landscape, and a fresh setting for Mab and Russell's horticultural interests. There, European and native plants and trees stood in dialogue with one another; the garden included fifty varieties of eucalypts, 'an orchard of fifty fruit trees, and some acres of lavender and geranium'.[26] Westerfield's garden combined the practical with the aesthetic, including both ornamental and productive elements. In addition to the large rose garden, the property housed a variety of native and exotic medicinal plants. Russell, a biochemist by training and an investor in essential oils, used extracts from medicinal plants to create vital drugs for the war effort during the 1940s.

While the Miegunyah and Westerfield gardens have been recognised as offering scope for Russell's experimental energies and explorations, little has been written on how they were an expression of Mab's creative vision or were used by Mab herself. She helped to preserve and extend the Miegunyah rose garden, which by 1958 included a clipped cypress hedge, a border of rosemary, classical urns and tall pines.[27] Mab was devoted to her garden at Miegunyah, and in addition to her own gardening practice oversaw a team of gardeners working there and took great pleasure in its offerings. Images abound of her among the flowers at Miegunyah and Westerfield, both enjoying the grounds and donning gardening apron and gloves and gripping secateurs to prune, pick and arrange flowers. Camilla Kelly recalled Mab's frequent use of the garden: 'she would run down to the garden for something ... she was interested in the garden & always picked her own flowers and arranged them in the house'.[28] As the head of the Miegunyah household and garden, she organised the orders to nurseries and florists. An entire room—decorated with Margaret Stones' botanical illustrations—was dedicated to flower arranging, and here Mab would oversee or participate in developing sophisticated ornamental flower designs for the various events held at the house.

In her garden making and use, Mab was continuing a tradition of elite white-settler women in constructing gardens and landscapes during the late nineteenth and early twentieth centuries. Holly Kerr Forsyth has explored this phenomenon, tracing the lives of women who helped to create their own 'visions of the Australian landscape' in the establishment and consolidation of the colonies and a new nation.[29] Despite women's participation in gardening and landscape design, the 'average home gardener' was almost always represented as a man: gardening required physical strength, mental aptitude and scientific knowledge, which were supposedly out of a woman's reach. Nevertheless, women were often actively engaged with the organisation, design and making of their gardens, acting as important abettors and mediators of culture and history in the process.

While men were associated with the utilitarian function of gardens, women were associated with their beauty. There existed a presumed affinity between women and flowers, so clearly displayed in rose-naming practices; as cultural historian Katie Holmes notes, 'femininity [was] aligned with the delicate style and perfume of the species she cultivated'.[30] In gardening magazines, women were depicted tending to their flower gardens and often became part of the garden display in images. Such associations persisted throughout the twentieth century: in 1964, 'Lady Grimwade's yellow rhododendrons' appeared in the *Australian Women's Weekly*.[31]

While decorative gardening was encouraged as a suitable feminine activity tied to the domestic sphere, gardening culture often blended public and private worlds, particularly in the case of competitions and open gardens. Mab expertly capitalised on the public reputation of the Miegunyah garden, opening it to the public on several occasions to raise money for the Fitzroy Mission Free Kindergarten.[32] She also attended and provided floral arrangements for other open garden charity events in Toorak. From 1952 to 1954 she attended three open gardens at Alice Creswick's mansion in Toorak; these included 'Floral Art Shows' and 'Rose Day' appeals to raise money for kindergartens.[33] While Victoria's Open Gardens Scheme was not formalised until the 1980s, open gardens were an important part of genteel women's community organising and philanthropy during Mab's lifetime. In the press, 'Melbourne hostesses' were associated with the decorative aspects of their gardens, particularly colourful flower arrangements, which reflected the prevailing association between gardening, domesticity and femininity. Yet Mab's productive use of the Miegunyah garden as a site for public participation, community organising and charity work redefined its purpose and signifies the unique relationship she had with the garden, and the influence she exerted in shaping its utility and public display.

Following spread, Mab gardening at Miegunyah, April 1913.

CIVIC HORTICULTURE

Victoria's culture of gardening developed into a flourishing civic infrastructure during the mid nineteenth century. By the early twentieth century, Mab and Russell were embedded in a statewide, national and international network of professional and amateur horticulturalists and botanists. This network reflected the strong association between horticulture and 'modern' civic identity during this time and provided Mab and Russell with an outlet for their fervent nationalism and conservationist impulses. Russell was a founding member of the Australian Forest League in 1912 and a member of the Melbourne Botanic Gardens Advisory Committee from 1923 to 1945, and was the president of the Royal Horticultural Society of Victoria (RHSV). Through their gardening networks, he and Mab extended their commitment to conservation and the preservation of Australian plants and wildlife. Indeed, while many white settlers drew upon a distinctly European understanding of the landscape, Mab and Russell were relatively attuned to the complexity and uniqueness of Australian plants and the need to conserve them. The couple worked with Percival St John, the systematist at Melbourne's Royal Botanic Gardens, to ensure the preservation of endangered flora in Victoria's high country.[34]

While men dominated Victorian horticultural societies during this period, Mab participated in the formal side of Victorian horticulture in various ways and played an active role in the conservation of native plants. She was a member and a patron of several horticultural institutions, including the RHSV, the Society for Growing Australian Plants, and the Native Plants Preservation Society of Victoria. Her influence in the horticultural community saw her opening the Royal Horticultural Society's spring show in 1946.[35] Held at Melbourne Town Hall, the show was advertised as the most 'interesting and comprehensive display' the RHSV had seen in twenty years, boasting an array of native and European flora from across the country. Air transport had opened the possibilities of establishing an 'interstate championship' for all seasonal flowers, including 'carnations from South Australia, wildflowers from Tasmania, and collections of lupins, tulips, pelargoniums, maples and hollies'.[36] The society claimed to have assembled the 'largest collection of gladioli, dahlias and vegetables ever exhibited in Australia'.[37] In her opening speech, Mab 'stressed the desirability of all societies combining and working together with the Royal Horticultural Society, so that there would be one paramount authority on horticulture in the State'.[38] In the following decades, her involvement in the RHSV cemented her membership of a community of amateur and professional horticulturalists that had existed in Victoria since the early days of colonisation.

The Victorian Horticultural Society was established in 1848 by the pioneer John Pascoe Fawkner and the superintendent of the Port Phillip District, Charles La Trobe, to bring together those interested in botany and horticulture. In 1885 the society was granted a royal charter by Queen Victoria and became the Royal Horticultural Society, joining several other horticultural and acclimatisation societies forming across Australia. While the annual shows of the RHSV initially provided enthusiasts with the opportunity to share and display their plants, flowers and produce to the public, over time they became competitive, with standardised judging.[39] Members of the RHSV wanted to develop a distinctly Victorian—and, later, Australian—gardening culture as part of their broader vision of transposing British culture to the colonies while adapting to the new environment. Indeed, in a speech made by Russell to the RHSV in 1948, he stated that 'Australia had never played its proper part in its contributions to gardens' as a country 'unsurpassed in its wonderful range of flowers'; it was 'time this natural blessing was properly developed'.[40] Mab's own vision for the RHSV as the 'paramount authority' of all horticultural societies in the state would be fulfilled over the course of the twentieth century: it became the umbrella organisation of hundreds of horticultural and botanic societies across Victoria.

•

Mab continued to preside over a flowering garden in the final decades of her life, and the maintenance of the Miegunyah grounds was a crucial part of her wish for the property. At a meeting in 1963 regarding the possible future of Miegunyah and its upkeep by the University of Melbourne, she insisted that 'the garden should be preserved in its natural state, with the assistance of the [university's] Botany School'.[41] Moreover, almost a third of the annual budget for the Miegunyah upkeep was allocated for the employment of a full-time gardener. Mab displayed a clear desire for the garden to be preserved as an artefact of Victorian gardening culture, and as an expression of her and Russell's lifelong devotion to it and to horticulture.

Conclusion

Lady Mabel Grimwade died on 6 September 1973 at the age of eighty-six. For eighteen years after her husband's death she had continued to live quietly at Miegunyah, accompanied by friends and family and with a small staff who tended to the house and gardens. She still travelled overseas but less frequently, and remained an active philanthropist and autodidact, attending the Fine Arts lectures of Professor Joseph Burke at the University of Melbourne and meetings of the National Gallery Society. In her final years she showed signs of mental deterioration, becoming 'detached and repetitive' in her old age'.[1] When she died, 'obsequies were respectful, and from those who knew her best, affectionate'.[2]

Following Mab's death, Miegunyah and its impressive contents became the Miegunyah Fund and Bequests, received by the University of Melbourne in 1973. The process of forming and instituting the Fund and Bequests was complicated and drawn out. In his will, Russell had outlined his and Mab's 'joint wishes' for their estates, with the specification that Mab would inherit the entire estate if she outlived him and that the University of Melbourne would be the primary beneficiary of the Grimwades' estates, reflecting their long commitment to the institution. In the final clause of his will, Russell had dictated his hopes for Miegunyah according to three stated 'principles': the property would become the headquarters of the Melbourne University Press (MUP), with the rear portions of the ground floor and the upstairs rooms kept as a residence for either the manager of MUP or the Professor of Fine Arts; the main ground-floor rooms were to be maintained as a museum; and the collection of Australiana books would be preserved as a 'collection for all time' and retained at Miegunyah as a reference library for students of Australian history.[3]

These provisions reflected both Russell's and Mab's intention to preserve Miegunyah as a memorial to a time and place, and to inspire future generations with its contents: Russell stated that it was the wish 'of my wife and myself that Miegunyah shall at all times be occupied and that it shall remain as far as possible as it has been in our lifetime as a representation of a way of life in an era that may be closing for all time'.[4] While he spoke for himself and Mab, she owned Miegunyah, and any clause in her husband's will regarding the property and its furnishings was subject to her wishes and had to be reflected in her own will.

Mab took on the responsibility for the Grimwades' estate in the wake of Russell's death. In her will, she bequeathed the sum of £40,000 to the university to be used 'primarily to assist in ensuring that Miegunyah is maintained and carried on in a proper manner'.[5] The possessions bequeathed by Mab from Miegunyah included 'all my furniture furnishings and pictures and all other personal chattels', leaving aside certain items such as jewellery, clothing and individual bequests. Pecuniary legacies were provided for family members, friends, employees and charities. Mab consolidated her commitment to the Fitzroy Mission Free Kindergarten with a gift of £1000; the Toorak Presbyterian Church received the same amount, while the Victorian Association of Braille Writers was given £250.

Mab dealt with the Miegunyah Bequests in an astute and perceptive manner, making amendments to the original bequest as stated in Russell's will to reflect her own wishes and the changing times. While most of Russell's wishes remained, she expressed doubts over the provision that the Professor of Fine Arts and the manager of the Melbourne University Press should live at Miegunyah, recording her change of mind:

> Since the death of my late husband it has been proposed that instead of portions of 'Miegunyah' being made available as a residence for the Manager of the Melbourne University Press or for the Professor of the Melbourne University School of Fine Arts it would be preferable for 'Miegunyah' to be used for the accommodation and entertainment of distinguished visitors to the said University and for the accommodation of the necessary staff.

Mab spoke for Russell and for herself: 'I am confident that the said proposal would commend itself to my late husband if he were still alive and it commends itself to me.' This new provision reflected a paper drawn up by Sir James Darling, a member of the University Council, after a meeting in May 1963 attended by Mab; relatives Andrew Grimwade and John Kelly; vice-chancellor of the University of Melbourne Sir George Paton; Sir Clive Fitts, Mab's medical advisor; and Sir Colin Syme, a trustee of Russell's estate and Mab's personal lawyer. At this meeting, a few suggestions were raised regarding the proposed uses of Miegunyah. It was suggested that the commercial and production facilities of MUP should remain in Carlton, while Miegunyah should house the editorial section of the Press. The proposal that made it into the will—that Miegunyah should provide accommodation for distinguished guests and visitors—led Mab to interject that the university would need to provide 'suitable silver' for guests since it was her 'present thinking' that the silver be bequeathed 'elsewhere'.[6] The preservation of Miegunyah's garden was central to Mab's wishes, and control of the annual budget for the maintenance of the property was to be given to a council or a board of trustees. She was adamant that this council be composed of members of both the Kelly and Grimwade families, a representative of the university, Sir James Darling and Clive Fitts.

Mab's careful deliberation over the will reflected her determination to preserve Miegunyah in its 'natural state', serving as testament to her life and to the time and place her home represented. Subsequently, it became apparent that the university could not fulfil the Grimwades' wishes for Miegunyah, and the property was sold in 1987. The proceeds of the sale became the Russell and Mab Grimwade Miegunyah Fund, which has been used to extend the Grimwades' interests within the university. While the sale of Miegunyah altered their vision for their extensive collection housed at the property, the proceeds have facilitated additional funding for Miegunyah's maintenance and preservation.

Miegunyah has been home to a succession of owners since Mab's passing, but it remains a physical legacy of her and Russell and the world they created for themselves. The Grimwade Collection, too, reflects their sense of duty to preserve and maintain many of the cultural artefacts of Australia's colonial and national history. Their bequeathed possessions were foundational to the university's cultural collections and have provided following generations with a vital source of materials that document Australia's colonial, political and cultural history.

Mab writing in the Miegunyah study, May 1966.

The role Mab played in the acquisition of art, decorative objects, furniture, botanical specimens and Australiana is subject to speculation. In her extensive investigation of the Grimwade Collection, Alisa Bunbury found Mab's presence difficult, although not impossible, to locate in the collection.[7] By weaving together speculation and fact, we can assume that she was part of its curation—her love of European and Australian art is reflected in the extensive assortment of oil paintings, illustrations and etchings; her fondness for flowers and floral arranging is embodied by a number of floral still lifes; a preference for antiques is manifest in Miegunyah's European porcelain figurines, English glassware and Chinese vessels; and several Scottie-dog ashtrays exemplify her devotion to her treasured pets.

The collection is now scattered across a range of University of Melbourne repositories, including the University Archives, the University Library's Special Collections, and the University Art Collection cared for by the Ian Potter Museum of Art. In May 2000 the University Council endorsed the allocation of $175,895 to the Ian Potter Museum of Art for rehousing and conserving the Grimwade collections.[8] Frances Lindsay, then deputy director of the National Gallery of Victoria, had suggested in her submission for funding to the University Council the previous year that a new catalogue be composed based on the research of Grimwade intern Laurelee MacMahon, focusing on Mab's life and 'the role she played in the acquisition of decorative objects'.[9] That project never came to fruition.

•

Distanced by only one generation from an Irish immigrant fleeing incarceration, Mab was the product of the possibilities for social mobility in the Antipodes. Born just before the dawn of the twentieth century, she grew up in a society marked by technological innovation, heightened national sentiment and fluctuating imperial ties. She inherited her position as a member of Melbourne's social elite and lived within the boundaries drawn for women of her class and status. It was a life so secure in its traditions that the upheavals of larger society tended to leave it undisturbed. Mab fulfilled her role as debutante, wife, hostess and Lady. She was not confined by these roles: she relished the logistics and creativity of event organisation, and used her status to extend her interests and advocate for the causes she believed in. Her social and cultural impact suggests a full and energetic life enriched with diverse and fulfilling pursuits.

Mab's choice to marry the industrious young man she met at Woolongoon in 1908 shifted the trajectory of her life. For forty-six years, she shared her life with her husband, developing a bond based on mutual devotion, common interests and a perceived duty to conserve and cultivate Australia's natural landscapes and cultural institutions. Together they built homes that were both sanctuaries and monuments; toured the world's golf courses, art centres and natural wonders; expanded their rich collections; and helped to shape the future of Victoria.

While Russell was undoubtably Mab's closest companion, tracing her various pursuits reveals a world with women at its centre. This was the realm of morning teas, charity events and hat shows, expensive gowns, countless administrative meetings, all-female sporting events, horticultural competitions and open gardens. It involved a community of women whose activities and work challenged the dichotomy between public and private spheres, privileging the knowledge and skill set required to organise both intimate gatherings and large-scale events. This social milieu was central to the functioning and maintenance of elite society, providing crucial opportunities for networking, the display of altruism and the extension of social status and cultural capital. In this milieu Mab was not only a participant but also an orchestrator and a leader. She excelled in positions of leadership and administration in many facets of her life. At eighteen she captained a girls' cricket team, and in later years she flourished in her role as president of the associates at the Royal Melbourne Golf Club. She was president of the Fitzroy Mission Free Kindergarten from about 1946 to at least 1955 and was a committee member and president of various fundraising committees and organisations.

Imbued with a sense of *noblesse oblige*, Mab dedicated much of her time to philanthropy and charity work, directing her altruistic energies to developing Victoria's social, cultural, civic and educational institutions. Her work in this field was inspired by a combination of an individual sense of responsibility and a broader conservative nationalism that shaped her worldview. This form of nationalism was common among Australia's upper classes, departing from radical anti-imperial nationalisms that emerged during the late nineteenth and early twentieth centuries and instead appreciating the benefits of belonging to the British Empire while acknowledging the distinctness of Australian society and culture. Indeed, Mab and her milieu embodied the symbiotic relationship between national and imperial identities within Australia and abroad.

Her social circle in Australia was at once an imprint of British aristocracy and a distinctly Australian elite, one that sought to create national institutions and practices that both reflected and departed from British traditions. This elite did not disrupt the social order—in fact, it reinscribed it. But in the process, it helped to create something new and distinct.

·

For decades, attempts have been made to recover Mab's inner world and her cultural impact. Such attempts have been met with silences and obstructions, many of which were enforced by Mab herself. In my own search for her through the extant traces of her life, I had a profound sense that she would have preferred an obscure place in the historical record, to remain in the shadows. The aim of this book has been to understand her social and cultural context, allowing her to act as a conduit to wider historical patterns and insights while maintaining her preference for privacy.

By delving into the world of Mab Grimwade, we learn something of the gendered dimensions of class in Australia, the strength of conservative nationalism during the early twentieth century, and the essential role of place making and the creation of 'home' in the composition of identity and the preservation of the past. There are absences in this story and much of Mab's interior life that remains elusive and unexplored, but my hope is that this book offers a scaffolding for future projects involving Mab, providing direction rather than a destination.

Acknowledgements

This book would not exist without the meticulous research of Juliet Flesch. Thank you, Juliet, for carefully scouring the archives in search of Mab and providing the foundations from which this book has grown. Parts of the first chapter of this book are based on an original text written by Juliet.

I am grateful to the team at Melbourne University Publishing, particularly Nathan Hollier, Cathryn Smith and Katie Purvis, for their insightful comments, guidance and patience.

Thank you to Alisa Bunbury for your valuable insights into Mab and Russell. Your assistance in collecting information, anecdotes and impressions of the elusive Mab has been indispensable to this project.

Thank you to the University of Melbourne Archives and Special Collections team, especially Sophie Garrett, Katie Wood, Georgina Ward, Alecia Cerreto, Jane Beattie and Silvia Paparozzi, for your assistance in procuring the archival resources and images of Mab that enrich this book.

Thank you to State Library Victoria, especially David Flegg, for your help in finding the protagonist of this story. I thank the Royal Melbourne Golf Club Archives for your assistance in providing information on the Mab Grimwade Cup.

Archives can only illuminate part of a whole. I wish to thank the family members and friends of Mab Grimwade, including Sir Andrew Grimwade, Camilla Kelly, Katrina Weatherly and Diana Hall, who provided inspiration, anecdotes and memories that filled out the picture of Mab presented in this book.

A special thankyou to Georgina Arnott for your generosity. I am indebted to you for your unwavering encouragement and support.

Thank you to Joy Damousi for your long-term mentorship and guidance.

Thank you to Catherine Gay for your expertise and your friendship.

To my family—Sue, Greg, Ed, Alex and our Jude—thank you. And to Miriam, Bernard, Chris and Betty.

Image Credits

page ii: Russell Grimwade, Mabel Grimwade in a gondola in Venice, 1 October 1927, black and white print, Sir Wilfrid Russell Grimwade and Lady Grimwade Collection, UMA 2002.0003.0163.

page viii: [Mab gardening at Miegunyah, October 1916.]

page xi: Arnold Shore, *Mabel Grimwade*, 1937, oil on cardboard, 81 × 56.5 cm, University of Melbourne Art Collection, Ian Potter Museum of Art, gift of the Russell and Mab Grimwade Bequest, 1973, accession no. 1973.0058.000.000.

1. Beginnings
[Studio portrait of Mabel Kelly 1902.]

Mab with party at Woolongoon, including cousins Violet and Gladys Weatherly and friend Sol McPherson, 9 September 1908, black and white print, 7 × 10 cm, Sir Wilfred Russell and Lady Grimwade Collection, UMA 2002.0003.00188.

Russell Grimwade, house and garden at Montalto, April 1909, black and white print, 7.5 × 10 cm, Sir Wilfred Russell and Lady Grimwade collection, UMA 2002.0003.00560.

Russell Grimwade, Mab with Dalziel and Agnes at Montalto, December 1926, black and white print, 7.3 × 10 cm, Sir Wilfred Russell and Lady Grimwade collection, UMA 2002.0003.00643.

Mabel Kelly to Gladys Weatherly, 4 October 1901. Weatherly Papers, State Library of Victoria, MS9617.

Russell Grimwade, Miegunyah, 10 August 1913, black and white print, 7.5 × 10 cm, Sir Wilfred Russell and Lady Grimwade collection, UMA 2002.0003.00432.

2. At Home
[Mab playing with young relative in Miegunyah gardens, 8 February 1931.]

['Miss Mabel Kelly' makes her debut, *Punch*, 1 June 1905.]

Russell Grimwade, Mab reading newspaper in Miegunyah garden, 5 April 1917, black and white print, Sir Wilfred Russell and Lady Grimwade collection, UMA 2002.0003.00704.

Russell Grimwade, Miegunyah, October 1933, black and white print, 8 × 12 cm, Sir Wilfred Russell and Lady Grimwade collection, UMA 2002.0003.00656.

Russell Grimwade, Mab on the steps of Miegunyah with young relative, 13 April 1918, black and white print, Sir Wilfred Russell and Lady Grimwade collection, UMA 2002.0003.00722.

Russell Grimwade, Miegunyah interior, black and white print, November 1931, Sir Wilfred Russell and Lady Grimwade collection, UMA 2002.0003.00715.

Miegunyah interior, Sir Andrew Grimwade Papers, Box 35, UMA.

Russell Grimwade, Mab in motor car at Miegunyah holding a Scottie dog, 16 January 1916, black and white print, Sir Wilfred Russell and Lady Grimwade collection, UMA 2002.0003.00722.

Mab with dog at Miegunyah, 24 June 1935, black and white print, 12 × 8 cm, Sir Wilfred Russell and Lady Grimwade collection, UMA 2002.0003.00557.

Russell Grimwade, a panoramic view of Westerfield, 18 January 1925, black and white print, 5.4 × 17.2 cm, Sir Wilfred Russell and Lady Grimwade collection, UMA 2002.0003.00239.

Russell Grimwade, Mab with Daryl and Joan Lindsay at Westerfield, 27 December 1925, black and white print, 7.2 × 10 cm, Sir Wilfred Russell and Lady Grimwade collection UMA 2002.0003.00151.

Russell Grimwade, Mab embroidering at Miegunyah, 25 February 1935, black and white print, Sir Wilfred Russell and Lady Grimwade collection, UMA 2002.0003.00718

Russell Grimwade, Mab with Scottish terrier at Westerfield, c. 1930, black and white print, Sir Wilfred Russell and Lady Grimwade collection, UMA 2002.0003.00890.

Russell Grimwade, Russell and Mab at Westerfield, 8 January 1928, black and white print, 10 × 7.2 cm, Sir Wilfred Russell and Lady Grimwade collection UMA 2002.0003.00223.

[Opposite, Mab and Russell at Westerfield, January 1928.]

Russell Grimwade, Mab and companion at Westerfield, 5 April 1930, black and white print, Sir Wilfred Russell and Lady Grimwade collection, UMA 2002.0003.00714.

3. Abroad
Russell Grimwade, Mab with friends Lorna and Dennis Sargood on the banks of the Loire, Tours, France, 7 November 1921, black and white print, 7.8 × 10.5 cm, Sir Wilfred Russell and Lady Grimwade Collection, UMA 2002.0003.00165.

Russell Grimwade, Mab winning a deck quoits competition on the RMS *Niagara*, July 1923, black and white print, 7.2 × 10 cm, Sir Wilfred Russell and Lady Grimwade Collection, UMA 2002.0003.00641.

Russell Grimwade, Mab seated on a rickshaw in Darjeeling, 6 March 1921, black and white print, 7.3 × 10.5 cm, Sir Wilfred

Russell and Lady Grimwade Collection, UMA 2002.0003.00473.

Russell Grimwade, portrait of Mab in London, 21 July 1921, black and white print, 10 × 7.8 cm, Sir Wilfred Russell and Lady Grimwade Collection, UMA 2002.0003.00338.

Russell Grimwade, Château de Chambord, France, 6 November 1921, black and white print, Sir Wilfred Russell and Lady Grimwade Collection, UMA 2002.0003.00708.

Russell Grimwade, Mab and others observing the eclipse, Coronado, California, 10 September 1923, black and white print, Sir Wilfred Russell and Lady Grimwade Collection, UMA 2002.0003.00709.

Russell Grimwade, Mab on donkey-back in Egypt, February 1927, black and white print, Sir Wilfred Russell and Lady Grimwade Collection, UMA 2002.0003.00711.

Russell Grimwade, Mab sightseeing in Cairo, Egypt, 15 February 1921, black and white print, Sir Wilfred Russell and Lady Grimwade Collection, UMA 2002.0003.00711.

Russell Grimwade, Mab on the Amalfi Coast, 17 March 1927, black and white print, Sir Wilfred Russell and Lady Grimwade Collection, UMA 2002.0003.00712.

Russell Grimwade, Mab 'under the olives', 5 April 1927, black and white print, Sir Wilfred Russell and Lady Grimwade Collection, UMA 2002.0003.00712.

Russell Grimwade, Mab with friends in Blinda, Algeria, 29 March 1927, black and white print, Sir Wilfred Russell and Lady Grimwade Collection, UMA 2002.0003.00712.

Russell Grimwade, Mab in private gardens with companion, Kyoto, Japan, 31 March 1936, black and white print, Sir Wilfred

Russell and Lady Grimwade Collection, UMA 2002.0003.00719.

Russell Grimwade, Mab reclining by a motor car with friends and stray dogs in Bolton, England, March 1932, black and white print, Sir Wilfred Russell and Lady Grimwade Collection, UMA 2002.0003.00715.

4. Philanthropy and Charity Work
'Model Hats Displayed', *The Age*, July 1951.

Russell Grimwade, 'Comical Dog Show' at Miegunyah, 14 November 1931, black and white print, Sir Wilfred Russell and Lady Grimwade Collection, UMA 2002.0003.00719.

Russell Grimwade, 'Comical Dog Show' at Miegunyah, 14 November 1931, black and white print, Sir Wilfred Russell and Lady Grimwade Collection, UMA 2002.0003.00719.

'International House Given Large Cheque', *The Argus*, 1 July 1953.

'Principles in the Ceremony', *The Age*, 4 June 1949.

5. The Mab Grimwade Cup
'Montalto Cricket Team', *Table Talk*, 20 April 1905.

Russell Grimwade, Mab playing golf at Miegunyah, 30 June 1918, black and white print, Sir Wilfred Russell and Lady Grimwade Collection, UMA 2002.0003.00705.

Russell Grimwade, Mab playing golf at Westerfield, 17 November 1929, black and white print, Sir Wilfred Russell and Lady Grimwade Collection, UMA 2002.0003.00714.

Unknown, Del Monte Links, California, 24 August 1924, black and white print, Sir Wilfred Russell and Lady Grimwade

Collection, UMA 2002.0003.00709.

'Women's Foursomes at Royal Melbourne', *The Herald*, 15 May 1933.

6. The Mab Grimwade Rose
Russell Grimwade, Mab gardening at Westerfield, October 1929, black and white print, Sir Wilfred Russell and Lady Grimwade Collection, UMA 2002.0003.00714.

Eric Timewell, the Mab Grimwade Rose, February 2014, colour photograph. Wikimedia Commons / CC BY-SA 3.0.

Russell Grimwade, view of the garden at Miegunyah, 30 September 1917, black and white print, 7 × 9.5 cm, Sir Wilfred Russell and Lady Grimwade Collection, UMA 2002.0003.00460.

Russell Grimwade, *Statue of Amanda*, University of Melbourne Property and Campus Services, not catalogued.

Russell Grimwade, Mab gardening at Westerfield, 27 December 1925, black and white print, Sir Wilfred Russell and Lady Grimwade Collection, UMA 2002.0003.00710.

Russell Grimwade, Mab gardening at Westerfield, 27 December 1925, black and white print, Sir Wilfred Russell and Lady Grimwade Collection, UMA 2002.0003.00710.

Russell Grimwade, Mab gardening at Miegunyah, April 1913, black and white print, Sir Wilfred Russell and Lady Grimwade Collection, UMA 2002.0003.00703.

Conclusion
Unknown, Mab writing in the Miegunyah study, 20 May 1966, courtesy John Poynter, Poynter Papers.

Notes

Introduction

1 George Kelly to Nell Wilson, Weatherly Papers, MS 9617/25-30, State Library Victoria.

2 Mabel Kelly was a wealthy Irish landowner who had inspired an eighteenth-century fiddle tune composed by a blind harpist, Turlough O'Carolan. The song is filled with Gaelic tropes, depicting Mabel as a fair-haired maiden and the 'love and interest of all young men'; see 'Appendix 1: "Mabel Kelly"', in Katrina Weatherly, *The Daddie of the Field: The Kelly Story from Ballinasloe to Barwidgee* (Streatham, Vic.: Katrina Weatherly, 2008), 392.

3 Camilla Kelly, 'Memories of Mab', written for Alisa Bunbury, May 2019. Held in the Grimwade research files, University of Melbourne Art Collection.

4 Certificate from the Royal Automobile Club of Victoria, Sir Russell and Lady Grimwade Papers, MS 1975.0089/16/14, University of Melbourne Archives.

5 The Elements of Home Nursing, Sir Russell and Lady Grimwade Papers, MS 1975.0089/16/12, University of Melbourne Archives.

6 Barbara W Tuchman, 'Biography as a Prism of History', Stephen B Oates (ed.), in *Biography as High Adventure: Life-Writers Speak on Their Art* (Amherst: The University of Massachusetts Press, 1986), 96.

1 Beginnings

1 The story of Mab and Russell's first meeting has been recorded in several publications: see JR Poynter, *Russell Grimwade* (Carlton, Vic.: Melbourne University Press at the Miegunyah Press, 1967), 97-8; Weatherly, *The Daddie of the Field*, 168-9.

2 Poynter, *Russell Grimwade*, 97.

3 Weatherly, *The Daddie of the Field*, 14-15.

4 Ibid., 14-15.

5 Ibid., 31.

6 See Michelle J Smith, Kristine Moruzi and Clare Bradford, *From Colonial to Modern: Transnational Girlhood in Canadian, Australian, and New Zealand Literature, 1840-1940* (Toronto: University of Toronto Press, 2018), 8.

7 Poynter, *Russell Grimwade*, 98.

8 'Obituary', *Malvern Standard*, 8 January 1910.

9 Graeme Davison, *The Rise And Fall of Marvellous Melbourne* (Carlton, Vic.: Melbourne University Publishing, 2014), 33-4.

10 Weatherly, *The Daddie of the Field*, 133.

11 The Toorak Heritage Citation Report on 687-689 Orrong Road states that George Colman bought the property in 1895; see 687-689 Orrong Road, Toorak Heritage Citation Report, Stonnington Thematic Environmental History (Carlton, Vic.: Context Pty Ltd, 2006). Katrina Weatherly gives the purchase date as July 1897: see Weatherly, *The Daddie of the Field*, 137.

12 Paul De Serville, *Pounds and Pedigrees: The Upper Class in Victoria, 1850-80* (South Melbourne: Oxford University Press, 1991), 147.

13 687-689 Orrong Road, Toorak Heritage Citation Report.

14 'Juvenile Costume Ball', *The Australasian*, 5 November 1898.

15 Laurelee MacMahon, 'Preface'. Held in the Grimwade research files, University of Melbourne Art Collection.

16 'Judicial and Law Notices', *The Argus*, 19 June 1935.

17 Mabel Kelly to Gladys Weatherly, 13 October 1901, Weatherly Papers, 1895, MS9617/27, State Library Victoria.

18 Mabel Kelly to Margaret Wilson, 26 September 1901, Weatherly Papers, 1895, MS9617/27, State Library Victoria.

19 Mabel Kelly to William Weatherly, 22 September 1901, Weatherly Papers, 1895, MS9617/27, State Library Victoria.

20 Mabel Kelly to Margaret Wilson, 26 September 1901, Weatherly Papers, 1895, MS9617/27, State Library Victoria.

21 It has also been suggested by family members that Mab may have attended Toorak College, although there is insufficient evidence for this claim.

22 Richard Peterson, *A Place of Sensuous Resort: Buildings of St Kilda and Their People* (Melbourne: St Kilda Historical Society, 2005), 27.

23 Craig Campbell and Helen Proctor, *A History of Australian Schooling* (Sydney: Allen & Unwin, 2014), 102.

24 Weatherly, *The Daddie of the Field*, 162.

25 'Melbourne Chatter', *The Bulletin*, 13 August 1908.

26 'Sidelights on Society', *Sunday Times*, 25 April 1909.

27 'Grimwade and Kelly', *Punch*, 21 October 1909.

28 Poynter, *Russell Grimwade*, 77.

29 Camilla Kelly, 'Memories of Mab'.

2. At Home

1 'Miss Mabel Kelly', *Punch*, 1 June 1905.

2 'At What Age Should a Girl Come Out?,' *Albury Banner and Wodonga Express*, 14 June 1901.

3 'Mrs. Wesley Hall's At Home', *The Australasian*, 10 June 1905; 'The Newsboy's Ball', *The Australasian*, 8 July 1905.

4 'Miss Mabel Kelly's Tea', *Table Talk*, 30 November 1905.

5 Jan Tent and Paul Geraghty, 'Miegunyah: From Bark Huts to Grand Houses and a Fiji Cane Farm', *Australian Journal of Linguistics* 40, no. 4 (December 2020): 428–43.

6 Miles Lewis, 'Miegunyah', Prahran Conservation Study, 1983.

7 'Party at Miegunyah', *The Australasian*, 16 November 1929.

8 Camilla Kelly, 'Memories of Mab'.

9 Poynter, *Russell Grimwade*, 100–1.

10 'After the Races', *The Herald*, 30 October 1937.

11 Camilla Kelly, 'Memories of Mab'.

12 'Westerfield', Victorian Heritage Database Report, Heritage Victoria, 2014.

13 See, for example, 'People, Parties', *The Age*, 13 June 1951; 'They Were Guests of the Governor-General', *The Age*, 5 November 1953; 'Woman's World', *The Herald*, 26 February 1954; 'Current Events Column', *The Argus*, 3 February 1954.

3. Abroad

1 Day Book, Proceedings of Mab & Russell, 1921, Sir Russell and Lady Grimwade Papers, MS 1975. 0089/6/3, University of Melbourne Archives. Further quotes in this section are from the same source.

2 Day Book, Proceedings of Mab & Russell, 1923, Sir Russell and Lady Grimwade Papers, MS 1975. 0089/6/3, University of Melbourne Archives. Further quotes in this section are from the same source.

3 Poynter, *Russell Grimwade*, 155.

4 Agnieszka Sobocinska, *Visiting the Neighbours: Australians in Asia* (Sydney: University of New South Wales Press, 2014), 170.

5 'Holiday Cruise', *The Age*, 25 September 1953.

6 Ibid.

7 Quoted in Poynter, *Russell Grimwade*, 307.

8 Mab Grimwade, Travel Journal, 1957, Sir Russell and Lady Grimwade Papers, MS 1975.0089/6/4, University of Melbourne Archives. Further quotes in this section are from the same source.

9 Travel Itinerary, Lady Grimwade, September 1960, Sir Russell and Lady Grimwade Papers, MS 1975.0089/16/2, University of Melbourne Archives.

10 Note from Wilmarth Sheldon Lewis to Mab Grimwade, September 1960, Sir Russell and Lady Grimwade Papers, MS 1975.0089/16/2, University of Melbourne Archives.

11 'Historic Housekeeping: A Short
Course', booklet, 15-21 September,
Sir Russell and Lady Grimwade Papers,
MS 1975.0089/16/2, University of
Melbourne Archives.

4. Philanthropy and Charity Work
1 'Royal Ascot Enclosure', *The Age*,
4 July 1951.
2 'Full House at Hat Show to Aid
Kindergarten', *The Argus*, 9 July 1951.
3 'People, Parties', *The Age*, 9 July 1951.
4 Shurlee Swain, 'Women and
Philanthropy in Colonial and Post-
Colonial Australia', in Kathleen
D McCarthy (ed.), *Women, Philanthropy,
and Civil Society*, Philanthropic
Studies, vol. 18 (Bloomington: Indiana
University Press, 2001), 161.
5 Melanie Oppenheimer, 'An Overview
of the Voluntary Principle in Australia:
Why the Past Matters', in Jeni
Warbuton and Melanie Oppenheimer
(eds), *Volunteers and Volunteering*
(Alexandria, NSW: Federation Press,
2000), 12; Barbara Lemon, 'In Her Gift:
Activism and Altruism in Australian
Women's Philanthropy 1880-2005'
(PhD thesis, University of Melbourne,
2008), 28 (italics in original).
6 Lemon, ibid.
7 'Brigade Comforts Issued', *Weekly Times*,
23 October 1915.
8 Lady Grimwade, various papers, 1964-
1966, Sir Russell and Lady Grimwade
Papers, MS 1975.0089/16/1, University
of Melbourne Archives.
9 Mary Matthews, 'Round Navy House',
The Australasian, 22 March 1941.
10 'An Original Idea', *The Herald*,
7 November 1931.
11 'International House Given Large
Cheque', *The Argus*, 1 July 1953.
12 'Brains in Her Hats', *The Argus*, 2 July
1955.
13 Helen Keller to Mab Grimwade,
22 March 1957, transcript, Foundation
for the Blind, Helen Keller Archive.
14 Lyndsay Gardiner, *The Free
Kindergarten Union of Victoria, 1908-80*
(Hawthorn, Vic.: Australian Council for
Educational Research, 1982), 1-2.
15 'Children of the Poor', *The Herald*,
14 October 1946.
16 'Kindergartens', *The Herald*, 22 October
1946.
17 'Annual Meeting at Fitzroy', *The Argus*,
2 October 1947.
18 'Principles in the Ceremony', *The Age*,
4 June 1949.
19 Swain, 'Women and Philanthropy in
Colonial and Post-Colonial Australia',
158.
20 Lady Grimwade's Speech at the
Opening of the Biochemistry Building,
1958, Sir Russell and Lady Grimwade
Papers, MS 1975.0089/5/6, University of
Melbourne Archives. Further quotes in
this section are from the same source.

5. The Mab Grimwade Cup
1 'Ladies Cricket', *The Age*, 20 March
1905.
2 'Montalto Cricket Team', *Table Talk*,
20 April 1905.
3 'Cricket', *The Independent*, 18 August
1906.
4 'Presbyterian Ladies' College',
The Australasian, 9 February 1907.
5 'Ladies' School, Oberwyl', *Launceston
Examiner*, 26 January 1886; 'Lawn-
Tennis', *The Argus*, 8 November 1909.
6 'Ladies Column: The Rights of
Women to Sport', *Adelaide Observer*,
14 November 1885.
7 Richard I Cashman and Amanda
Weaver, *Wicket Women: Cricket &
Women in Australia* (University of New
South Wales Press, Randwick, 1991), 35.
8 Fiona Skillen, 'Woman and the Sport
Fetish: Modernity, Consumerism
and Sports Participation in Inter-War
Britain', *International Journal of the
History of Sport* 29, no. 5, 2012, 751-2.
9 Travel Diary, Day Book, 5 February
1921-16, March 1927, Sir Russell
and Lady Grimwade Papers, MS
1975.2002/5/6/3/88 142, University of
Melbourne Archives. Further quotes in
this section are from the same source.

10 'The Game of Golf', *Geelong Advertiser*, 29 August 1894.

11 'Golf', *The Australasian*, 24 June 1893.

12 'The Melbourne Golf Club: Opening of the Caulfield Links', *The Argus*, 6 July 1891.

13 G Mansfield, *A History of Golf in Victoria* (Melbourne: Victorian Golf Association, 1987), 58.

14 June Senyard, 'The Imagined Golf Course: Gender Representations and Australian Golf', *International Journal of the History of Sport* 15, no. 2, 1998: 164.

15 Marion K Stell, *Half the Race: A History of Australian Women in Sport* (North Ryde, NSW: Collins/Angus & Robertson, 1991), 61.

16 Fiona McLachlan, 'It's Boom Time! (Again): Progress Narratives and Women's Sport in Australia', *Journal of Australian Studies* 43, no. 1, 2019: 7–21.

17 Mansfield, *A History of Golf in Victoria*, 65.

18 The Mab Grimwade Cup, Royal Melbourne Golf Club, Black Rock, biographical notes for the Royal Melbourne Golf Club. Held in the Grimwade research files, University of Melbourne Art Collection.

19 'Club Reports', *The Argus*, 11 October 1930.

20 'Golf Associates' Gossip', *Table Talk*, 28 November 1931.

21 'Miss Susie Tolhurst', *WA Amateur Sports*, 15 April 1932.

22 'From Women's Tees', *Weekly Times*, 31 July 1937.

23 Tilley Govanstone and Andrew Govanstone, *The Women Behind the Roses: An Introduction to Alister Clark's Rose-Namesakes 1915–1952* (Kenthurst, NSW: Rosenberg, 2010), 189.

24 'Women's Foursomes at Royal Melbourne', *The Herald*, 15 May 1933.

25 'Golf Associates Entertained at Royal Melbourne', *The Argus*, 6 April 1935.

26 Greg Ryan, '"They Came to Sneer, and Remained to Cheer": Interpreting the 1934–35 England Women's Cricket Tour to Australia and New Zealand', *International Journal of the History of Sport* 33, no. 17, 2016: 2127–8.

6. The Mab Grimwade Rose

1 In a botanical context, a sport is a genetic mutation that causes a plant to produce a stem or branch with different characteristics from the rest of the plant.

2 See: 2 1/22 88 142—Correspondence (inward and outward) re. 'Mrs Russell Grimwade' rose, developed by WH Griffiths (Miegunyah gardener). Correspondents include WA Stewart (Hon. Secretary), The National Rose Society of Victoria, 27 September 1937 – 13 January 1938, Sir Russell and Lady Grimwade Papers, 1975.0089/16/9, University of Melbourne Archives.

3 Historian John Poynter suggests that the rose bearing Mab's name was bred at Westerfield in 1937, although there is uncertainty about this date. The Australian Women's Register suggests that Alister Clark bred the rose.

4 Alister Clark, *The Australian Rose Annual* (Melbourne: Mitchell & Casey, 1937), 24. Proceeds from the rose's sale were donated to the National Rose Society of Victoria.

5 'While I Remember (Rose)', *The Herald*, 13 April 1937.

6 'New Australian Roses in Gift List of Mr. Alister Clark', *The Argus*, 6 April 1937.

7 'Gardening Notes: New Australian Roses', *The Australasian*, 22 May 1937.

8 'Roses, Easter Bridges and Ballet Girls', *The Advertiser*, 13 April 1938.

9 'Gardening Notes', *West Australian*, 22 July 1938.

10 'National Rose Show', *The Age*, 18 April 1939.

11 'Gardening Notes: The Australian Rose Annual', *The Australasian*, 16 July 1938.

12 TR Garnett, *Man of Roses: Alister Clark of Glenara and His Family* (Kenthurst, NSW: Kangaroo Press, 1990).

13 Ibid., 52-4.
14 Simon Morley, *By Any Other Name: A Cultural History of the Rose* (London: OneWorld Publications, 2021), 2-3.
15 Ibid., 8-9.
16 Govanstone and Govanstone, *The Women Behind the Roses*.
17 'Controversy over Clark Memorial', *The Argus*, 21 February 1949.
18 Katie Holmes, Susan K Martin and Kylie Mirmohamadi, *Reading the Garden: The Settlement of Australia* (Carlton, Vic.: Melbourne University Publishing, 2008), 79.
19 Ibid., 79, 189.
20 Poynter, *Russell Grimwade*, 90.
21 Katja Wagner, 'An Architectural Palimpsest', *University of Melbourne Collections* 24, 2019: 48-54.
22 Peter Watts and National Trust of Australia (Victoria), *Historic Gardens of Victoria: A Reconnaissance* (Melbourne: Oxford University Press, 1983).
23 Holly Kerr Forsyth, *Remembered Gardens: Eight Women and Their Visions of an Australian Landscape* (Carlton, Vic.: Melbourne University Publishing, 2008), 196.
24 Cited in JR Poynter and Benjamin Keir Thomas, *Miegunyah: The Bequests of Russell and Mab Grimwade* (Carlton, Vic.: The Miegunyah Press, 2015), 111.
25 'Garden Plans and Planting for Spring', *Australian Women's Weekly*, 9 July 1958.
26 Poynter, *Russell Grimwade*, 137-9.
27 'Garden Plans and Planting for Spring'.
28 Camilla Kelly, Memories of Mab.
29 Forsyth, *Remembered Gardens*, 1.
30 Holmes, Martin and Mirmohamadi, *Reading the Garden*, 89.
31 'Rhododendrons', *Australian Women's Weekly*, 1 April 1964.
32 'Garden Open', *The Herald*, 28 October 1946.
33 'In Town and Out', *The Herald*, 1 October 1951; 'Flower Arrangements in Home Setting', *The Age*, 25 October 1952; 'Floral Art Will Aid Kindergartens', *The Age*, 8 October 1954.
34 Poynter, *Russell Grimwade*, 300.
35 'Spring Flower Show', *The Argus*, 30 October 1946.
36 'Finish of a Garden Depends on Details', *The Herald*, 30 October 1946.
37 'Both Town Halls for Flower Show,' *The Herald*, 18 March 1948.
38 'Spring Show', *The Age*, 2 November 1946.
39 Marjorie Porter (ed.), *A Seed Is Planted: A History of the Royal Horticultural Society of Victoria 1848-2014* (Melbourne: Royal Horticultural Society of Victoria, 2014).
40 'Huge Blooms at R.H.S. Show', *The Age*, 20 March 1948.
41 Poynter and Thomas, *Miegunyah: The Bequests of Russell and Mab Grimwade*, 82.

Conclusion

1 Camilla Kelly, 'Memories of Mab'.
2 Poynter and Thomas, *Miegunyah: The Bequests of Russell and Mab Grimwade*, 82.
3 Wilfred Russell Grimwade, Will and Codicil, PROV VPRS 7591/P0 Wills, Unit 114, 498/777, 9 September 1953, 7-8.
4 Ibid.
5 Mabel Louise Grimwade, Will and Codicil, PROV VPRS 7591/p0 wills, Unit 391, 763/639, 2 June 1961, 3. Further quotes in this section are from the same source.
6 Poynter and Thomas, *Miegunyah: The Bequests of Russell and Mab Grimwade*, 81-2.
7 Alisa Bunbury (ed.), *Pride of Place: Exploring the Grimwade Collection* (Carlton, Vic.: The Miegunyah Press, 2020), xiii.
8 Poynter and Thomas, *Miegunyah: The Bequests of Russell and Mab Grimwade*, 175.
9 Ian Potter Museum of Art, Submission for Funding to the Miegunyah Fund Committee, January 1999, Sir Andrew Grimwade Papers, MS 1997.0095-2006.0040/35/39/4, University of Melbourne Archives.

Index

This book was designed and
typeset by Pfisterer + Freeman
The text was set in 8½ point
Galaxie Copernicus with 14½ points of leading
The text was printed on 120 gsm woodfree
This book was edited by Katie Purvis